Dedication

In gratitude for many wonderful Sunday School teachers, including Mrs. Bailey, Dale Clayton, Larry Huff, Dick Morris, and Phil Moore.

And in gratitude to Michelle Morris, who made this book possible.

Kevin Slimp
Publisher, Market Square Books

Royalties from *More Favorite Sunday School Lessons* go to support the work of Project Transformation® Arkansas.

For more information, visit:

projecttransformation.org/arkansas/

More Favorite Sunday School Lessons

Adult Sunday School Lessons by Clergy
of the Arkansas Conference

Michelle Morris

and friends from the Arkansas Conference
of the United Methodist Church

Market Square
BOOKS

More Favorite Sunday School Lessons

Adult Sunday School Lessons by Clergy of the Arkansas Conference

©2024 Market Square Publishing, LLC

books@marketsquarebooks.com
141 N. Martinwood, Suite 103-2 Knoxville, Tennessee 37923

ISBN: 978-1-950899-86-9

Printed and Bound in the United States of America
Cover Illustration & Book Design ©2024 Market Square Publishing, LLC

Compiled by Michelle Morris
Editor: Sheri Carder Hood
Post-Process Editor: Ken Rochelle
Design: Kevin Slimp

All rights reserved. No part of this book may be reproduced in any manner without written permission except in the case of brief quotations included in critical articles and reviews. For information, please contact Market Square Publishing, LLC.

Scripture quotations used with permission from:

CEB
Scripture quotations from the COMMON ENGLISH BIBLE. © Copyright 2011 COMMON ENGLISH BIBLE. All rights reserved. Used by permission. (www.CommonEnglishBible.com).

NRSVUE
Scripture quotations taken from the New Revised Standard Version Updated Edition. Copyright © 2021 National Council of Churches of Christ in the United States of America. Used by permission. All rights reserved worldwide.

NIV
Scriptures marked NIV are taken from the NEW INTERNATIONAL VERSION (NIV): Scripture taken from THE HOLY BIBLE, NEW INTERNATIONAL VERSION ®. Copyright© 1973, 1978, 1984, 2011 by Biblica, Inc.™. Used by permission of Zondervan.

MES
THE MESSAGE: THE BIBLE IN CONTEMPORARY ENGLISH (MES): Scripture taken from THE MESSAGE: THE BIBLE IN CONTEMPORARY ENGLISH, copyright©1993, 1994, 1995, 1996, 2000, 2001, 2002. Used by permission of NavPress Publishing Group

Contents

Lesson 1: Zeke Allen 1
  A Simple Guide to a Profound Faith

Lesson 2: Jacob Lynn 17
  Won't You Be My Neighbor?

Lesson 3: Michelle Morris 31
  God Designed Diversity

Lesson 4: Dan Read 45
  Reaching the Least, Last, and Lost

Lesson 5: Michael Roberts 55
  Love Abiding

Lesson 6: LaToya Juanita Shepherd and Mike McSpadden ... 71
  Savior, Like A Shepherd, Lead Us

Lesson 7: Melanie Tubbs 85
  The God of Hagar

Lesson 8: Bill Sardin 97
  Voice to the Voiceless

Bonus Lesson: Walter Cross 113
  There is Yet Hope

Lesson 1

A Simple Guide to a Profound Faith:
Three Simple Rules as a Guide to Putting Faith into Action while Living in Community

Lesson by Zeke Allen

About the Lesson Writer:

Zeke is the senior pastor at First United Methodist Church of Arkadelphia, Arkansas. He has served in the United Methodist Church since 1996, beginning with fourteen years of youth ministry and then transitioning to pastoral ministry, first as a local pastor and then as an elder in full connection.

Scripture Lesson:
James 2:14-26

> *What good is it, my brothers and sisters, if you say you have faith but do not have works? Can faith save you? If a brother or sister is naked and lacks daily food, and one of you says to them, "Go in peace; keep warm and eat your fill," and yet you do not supply their bodily needs, what is the good of that? So faith by itself, if it has no works, is dead.*

> *But someone will say, "You have faith and I have works." Show me your faith without works, and I by my works will show you my faith. You believe that God is one; you do well. Even the demons believe—and shudder. Do you want to be shown, you senseless person, that faith without works is barren? Was not our ancestor Abraham justified by works when he offered his son Isaac on the altar? You see that faith was active along with his works, and faith was brought to completion by the works. Thus*

the scripture was fulfilled that says, "Abraham believed God, and it was reckoned to him as righteousness," and he was called the friend of God. You see that a person is justified by works and not by faith alone. Likewise, was not Rahab the prostitute also justified by works when she welcomed the messengers and sent them out by another road? For just as the body without the spirit is dead, so faith without works is also dead.

James 2:14-26 (NRSV)

Introduction

I believe most people have the best of intentions most of the time. We generally want to thrive in our lives and wish for others to do the same. There can be a disconnect, though, between intent and reality. This is true in both secular and sacred living. We are so good at over-complicating our lives in almost every arena of life. I have come to believe more and more that, while we have more information at our ready than ever before, we have diminished in our collective wisdom as a people.

My dad was a practical wisdom guru. I was forever amazed at how he knew so much about all kinds of things. He had an inspiring grasp of how things worked and, in turn, a great knack for fixing almost anything. I cherish the moments when he taught me how something worked or how to repair something. These practical life lessons have helped shape my own understanding and wisdom and prodded me to search for more wisdom in our world. Amid this search, I have learned to love videos that show "hacks" on how to do things easily and quickly. I often think, "How did I not know this?" Truth is, we over-complicate life all too often, and more often than not, there are better ways to do what we do.

This tendency and trend of over-complication has carried unabated into faith and faith practice throughout the arc of Christendom. How often have Christians—and especially Christian leaders—majored in the minors, leaving themselves and others lost in proverbial weeds? This tendency tracks throughout history, often with unintended hazard and division. In this lesson, I invite you to consider some guardrails that help me stay focused as I seek to put my faith into action. We will look at this through James 2:14-26 and John Wesley's *Three Simple Rules*.

Before that journey, let us look briefly at the continued struggle between two foci in faith: orthodoxy and orthopraxy.

The Pull Between Orthodoxy and Orthopraxy

What is more important: believing the right things or putting your faith into practice in the right ways? This single question unveils an eternal struggle within individual faith and within the greater church. Orthodoxy is the theological study concerned with right belief. Orthopraxy is the theological study concerned with having correct conduct/ action. These two areas of study are often in tension with one another. This reality comes into focus when we look at the book of James as a whole, especially with the well-known verse of James

2:26: "… faith without works is dead." We can safely say that James has had a rocky relationship with people of faith throughout the church's history.

Many early church leaders sought to exclude the book of James from the biblical canon because of doubts surrounding its authorship. Likewise, reformers also took issue with it. Martin Luther described the book as a "letter of straw" because "he did not think James places enough emphasis on grace and places the wrong emphasis on justification by works."[1] With Luther's laser focus on sola fide (faith alone), his perspective on the book of James comes as no surprise. One can draw a stark contrast between Luther's view of James and John Wesley's view of James' epistle. In his journal, Wesley describes James as a "remedy against the general temptation of leaving off good works in order to increase faith."[2] In his sermon "The Mystery of Iniquity," Wesley notes that when James wrote his letter, "that grand pest of Christianity, a faith without works, was spread far and wide; filling the Church with a 'wisdom from beneath,' which was 'earthly, sensual, devilish,' and which gave rise, not only to rash judging and evil speaking, but to 'envy, strife, confusion, and every evil work.'"[3]

In my almost thirty years of full-time ministry within

---

[1] O. Wesley Allen, Jr., *The Preacher's Bible Handbook* (Westminster John Knox Press, September 2019), 333.

[2] John Wesley, *Works,* June 5, 1741.

[3] John Wesley, *Sermon 61, "The Mystery of Iniquity."*

the United Methodist Church, I have come to believe that the epistle of James is the most Methodist of all the epistles. We are a people who incessantly seek to put our faith into action in the world in meaningful, transformative ways. This reality shines forth in our staunch commitment to missions, works of justice, and works of peace. There is, however, a great possibility for imbalance if we overemphasize works. I have experienced people of faith who engage in works of faith as a means to merit divine favor. Most often, this is a subversive theological framework, but it is present, nonetheless. An overemphasis on works is an affront to God's grace and the gifted nature of our relationship with God through Jesus Christ. These two—orthodoxy and orthopraxy—must be held in a creative tension as we strive for balance.

The United Methodist Book of Discipline ¶102 reads, "No motif in the Wesleyan tradition has been more constant than the link between Christian doctrine and Christian living. Methodists have always been strictly enjoined to maintain the unity of faith and good works through the means of grace."[4] More than just advocating a core theme of Wesleyan tradition, this motif of balancing Christian doctrine and Christian living is a wholly Christian endeavor and one with which all people of faith wrangle and wrestle.

---

[4] *The United Methodist Book of Discipline* (The United Methodist Publishing House, 2012) ¶102.

James 2:14-26

The book of James has evoked mixed sentiments among Christians through the ages. It is helpful to bring into focus the book as a whole. "The primary focus of James is to offer wisdom to members of the community of faith so they can master things that distract them from fulfilling God's purposes."[5] James offers a meal of practical wisdom whereby people are invited to put their faith into action and calls Christians to an honest and unvarnished life of faith. I have come to believe that faith without action is simply misplaced faith, a viewpoint which is lifted up in James as a whole and specifically in our scripture passage from James 2:14-26.

Three Simple Rules as Guardrails for Putting Faith into Action

John Wesley developed the *Three Simple Rules* to guide people practicing faith within community. In Wesley's time—and in ours today—people of faith need all possible helpful tools at their disposal to encourage them to live a life of faith. *The United Methodist Book of Discipline* frames the *Three Simple Rules* by saying:

> It is therefore expected of all who continue therein that they should continue to evidence their desire of salvation, First: By doing no harm, by avoiding evil of every kind ...; Secondly: By ... doing good of every possible sort, and, as far as possible, to all ...; Thirdly: By attending upon the ordinances of God.[6]

---

[5] Allen, *The Preacher's Bible Handbook*, 334.

[6] *The United Methodist Book of Discipline*, ¶102.

These rules have been further simplified into the following:

1. Do No Harm
2. Do Good
3. Stay in Love with God

These *Three Simple Rules* have great potential as guardrails to help us navigate the often-treacherous waters of daily life and faith. In a world that seems bent on over-complication, the *Three Simple Rules* come to us as a breath of fresh, simple air. Let's look more closely at each of them and how they intersect with James 2.

1. Do No Harm

Think, for a moment, how our world might be transformed if this simple rule was at the forefront of how we interact or do business with one another. Practicing Wesley's directive to "Do no harm" challenges our tendencies to focus on navel-gazing and self-centeredness. Edified within this simple rule is the pursuit of "Loving your neighbor as yourself" (Mark 12:31). To do no harm invites us to move beyond ourselves as we think and act toward the well-being and benefit of others. In 2020, church leaders lifted up this directive as the COVID-19 pandemic swept through our country. I heard many communicating to their local congregations that in an attempt to do no harm, "We are online only this week," or, "We will continue to wear masks," etc. Truth be told, many churches took it on the chin for this stance and practice. Some people left our churches to go to other churches that went on as usual, operating like there was no pandemic at all. That was difficult for leaders trying to work to do no harm. This practice is not for the weak. When we work to do no harm, it is incredibly challenging.

Consequences — everything has them! In his book *Three Simple Rules*, Rueben Job intuitively writes that when we think about doing no harm, "We have time and space to think about consequences before a word is spoken or an action is taken."[7] Employing the ethical and relational guardrail of doing no harm helps us think through consequences and invites us to reflect on possible outcomes. In leadership, this is incredibly helpful and affords one insight into the implications of decision-making.

Inaction can actively do harm. James 2:14-15 is the biblical equivalent to the modern sentiment of someone offering "thoughts and prayers." How often do we speak to things that need to be done (checking on someone, missional need, prayer for someone struggling, affirming statement for someone doing great work, etc.), but we do not act on those urgings? A colleague often quipped the familiar saying, "The road to hell is paved with good intentions." They were so right. We are often guilty of intending to help someone or intending to make a call to check on someone, but then we never do. That

---

[7] Rueben P. Job, Three Simple Rules, A Wesleyan Way of Living (Abingdon Press, 2007), 22.

is an avenue where we do harm to one another. Often, it is our inaction—both in word and deed—that inflicts harm on others. Intentionally trying to do no harm also involves a prodding to be people who stand up and speak out when there is injustice or need. This ethic moves us out of a "thoughts and prayers" posture into an active faith that seeks to bring about transformation.

2. Do Good

Look again at James 2:15-16. We are all guilty, in varying degrees, of being able to identify injustice, oppression, need, and issues only to then do nothing to address the problem beyond talking. This human phenomenon rings through history. The simple rule to "Do Good" invites us to reframe life and faith in a way that prods us into action. It confronts the temptation to lead lip-service lives of faith and provokes us to "do."

The saying, "Do all the good you can, by all the means you can, in all the ways you can, in all the places you can, at all the times you can, to all the people you can, as long as ever you can," is a helpful one. While this saying is often attributed to Wesley, he most likely didn't say it, but I advocate he certainly could have. It is exactly what our second simple rule gets at. To seek to do good is to strive to put faith into action, bringing about good in our lives, community, and world. James 2 lifts up that "faith without works is dead." This begs the question, What is this "work" we are supposed to be doing? This simple rule frames it nicely for us.

I daily seek to do good through an unlikely and grossly underrated practice: kindness. Many people mistake kindness within others as a sign of weakness. Some of the strongest people I have ever met are also some of the kindest. Extending kindness to others as a practice of "doing good" is often incredibly hard and almost always inconvenient. However, through acts of kindness, I have seen the hardest hearts soften and the most guarded individuals transformed into advocates of kindness and love. We mustn't underestimate the power of this guardrail practice of doing good. Henry David Thoreau writes, "The Devil finds work for idle hands." When we fail to put our faith into action, we invite a myriad of struggles and strife. When we seek to do good, we actively seek ways to participate in the unfolding of God's kingdom in our midst here and now. When we frame our day's activities as opportunities to do good, we hold the potential to transform ourselves and others and invite a unique openness in our lives to the empowering, transforming work of God.

There is also the mystery of reciprocity when it comes to the practice of doing good. For example, I have had the privilege of attending and leading many mission trips through my years of ministry. A few of those trips were with Amore Ministries in the surrounding areas around Juarez, Mexico. A group of youth and adult volunteers would construct a two-room house from start to finish in five days without power tools. When we arrived, our clients often lived in a makeshift house made of old pallets and cardboard. At the onset of each trip, I always felt a sense of hope that our work would make a difference in the lives of others, and I believe it did in many ways. However, there is also a missional reciprocity that occurs. With each mission trip, I have been incredibly transformed and blessed. The sheer joy, even amid such hard living that these people had, challenged my affluent bias on success and happiness. I continually found myself drawn into places of profound hope and steadfast joy as I served. I believe there is a counterintuitive, mystical reciprocity to the work of doing good.

When we move outside our self-centered frame of reference and seek to do good toward others, there holds a powerful potential for blessing and transformation. Think of how our agendas, calendars, and to-do lists might change if we intentionally sought out and prioritized the mission to do good. When we reframe our agendas and to-dos of the day through the lens of striving to do good, it holds the potential to transform our lives and world.

3. Stay in Love with God

Wesley's original third simple rule was to "Attend to the ordinances of God." Thankfully, to accommodate our more modern context, the wording for the third simple rule is interpreted as "To stay in love with God." For Wesley, attending to the ordinances of God is how we, people of faith, nurture our relationship with God and one another. While the first rule establishes a moral imperative as a guardrail and the second rule establishes a missional guardrail, the third simple rule seeks to establish a motivational and inspirational guardrail for people of faith. It attempts to get at the foundational question of Christians always and everywhere: "Why do we do what we do?"

I feel confident that part of the response to this question should include love. The verse in 1 John 4:19 speaks to this reality: "We love because God first loved us." Throughout the corpus of Christ's teaching, along with the apostles that follow, we have a foundational emphasis on love as a Christian response. Disclaimer: the church has often leveraged guilt as a motivator for behavioral modification and financial gain. This simple rule confronts that reality and invites us to ground our lives primarily in God's love.

Think for a moment about the person and example of Rahab lifted up in our James passage. Rahab's love and concern for the others extends beyond her people as she welcomes the foreign spies into her house, granting them a safe haven and protection. How many times have we limited the confines of God's call on our lives to love as we choose to love only those we know? Rahab sets aside her own people's cultural and religious beliefs and opens up to strangers who bear witness to a new God doing new things. Rahab's hospitality is so profound in the arc of Israel's settling of the Promised Land that she is lifted up in the genealogical line of Jesus himself. We mustn't miss this profound reality that Rahab is included in the Messianic line of Jesus. As we strive to stay in love with God, this should remind us that we must be vigilantly open to whenever and wherever opportunities to love present themselves.

How do we stay in love with God? Wesley emphasized that one should worship God publicly, fast, pray, study scripture, and partake of Holy Communion to do this. Wesley and Methodists have emphasized Christian disciplines as vital to Christian discipleship. If we reframe Christian practices and disciplines through the lens of "staying in love with God," we will be recentered in transformational ways. For instance, how might your study of scripture be reframed if you were to approach it as a means by which you are staying in love with God? How might Holy Communion be reframed as a relational event whereby you and God are in a mystical exchange of mutual love for one another as you offer confession, affirm faith, and receive nourishment?

The motivational faith guardrail of staying in love with God invites participation in the ongoing and unfolding love story between God and God's people. I now believe the greatest concern across the biblical witness is relationship. The ongoing "crisis" in the religious and secular realm continues to revolve around relationship. This is no coincidence and is, in part, why the teachings and stories of the Bible still hold so much power, even within the contemporary realm. Our struggles with relationship transcend time. The simple rule to strive to stay in love with God is an invitation to find a better way, relationally, in our lives. It seeks to ground our actions as manifestations of our love of God and love of neighbor. In addition, striving for this third simple rule prompts us to strive to love ourselves more fully as God loves us. Think of the incredible transformational power we would all experience if we realigned our lives and agendas with the faithful pursuit to stay in love with God daily. Think of the powerful witness we would bring to a world so relationally fractured and taught to be individually focused. This third simple rule offers us a motivational guardrail to help guide us as we strive to act in faith daily.

Conclusion

We over-complicate life and faith as individuals and as the church. Also, we are guilty of talking and not acting. James 2:14-26 and Wesley's *Three Simple Rules* provide a foundation to help us do better. We need simple guardrails to help guide us towards lives of purpose as people of faith. "Do No Harm" offers a moral imperative guardrail for us to frame our actions. "Do Good" offers a missional guardrail for us to use as we think about how to act on our faith in meaningful and transformative ways. Lastly, "Stay in Love with God" offers us a motivational guardrail to help us focus on why we do what we do. These are simple, precious tools for people to live faithfully as individuals and in community with one another.

Reflection Questions:

What is the most important moral guide for you as a person of faith? What do you see as your faith guardrails?

How do you see the tension of focusing on either orthodoxy or orthopraxy lived out in modern-day?

In what ways have you seen people of faith or the church actively do harm?

How would the church or society (on whatever scale you imagine) be transformed if "Do no harm" was the primary tenet of decision-making and practice?

How might your priorities and decision-making change if you committed to the practice of "Do no harm"?

How might your life be transformed if you intentionally sought to "Do Good" at least once each day?

If one person in your life were the poster child for prioritizing doing good, who would it be? Share why you thought of this person.

What is one mission or ministry that you believe prioritizes the work to do good?

In the context of faith, why do you do the things you do?

Lesson 2

Won't You Be My Neighbor?

Lesson by Jacob Lynn

About the Lesson Writer:

Jacob Lynn is the senior pastor at Cabot United Methodist Church in Cabot, Arkansas. Jacob has served as a pastor in the Arkansas Annual Conference for fourteen years, serving churches in Hot Springs, Little Rock, White Hall, and Rector. Jacob holds a Master's of Divinity from Saint Paul School of Theology.

Scripture Lesson:
Luke 14:15-23:

One of the dinner guests, on hearing this, said to him, "Blessed is anyone who will eat bread in the kingdom of God!" Then Jesus said to him, "Someone gave a great dinner and invited many. At the time for the dinner he sent his slave to say to those who had been invited, "Come; for everything is ready now." But they all alike began to make excuses. The first said to him, "I have bought a piece of land, and I must go out and see it; please accept my regrets." Another said, "I have bought five yoke of oxen, and I am going to try them out; please accept my regrets." Another said, "I have just been married, and therefore I cannot come." So the slave returned and reported this to his master. Then the owner of the house became angry and said to his slave, "Go out at once into the streets and lanes of the town and bring in the poor, the crippled, the blind, and the lame." And the slave said,

"Sir, what you ordered has been done, and there is still room." Then the master said to the slave, "Go out into the roads and lanes, and compel people to come in, so that my house may be filled."

Luke 14:15-23 (NRSV)

On a beautiful warm day in May, my cell phone rang as I pulled into the driveway of our new house in Bryant, Arkansas. I looked at my phone, and the caller ID said, "Bishop Gary Mueller." Not knowing if this call was good or bad, I thought, "Oh, I better take this." As a United Methodist pastor, the fate of my career can feel like it lies in the bishop's hands. So I reluctantly answered, "Heh...hello."

This was 2013, and I was finishing seminary and transitioning into my first full-time pastoral appointment. As I put the phone to my ear and listened, the bishop told me about an incredible opportunity. Bishop Mueller said he wanted to nominate me to participate in a program called "The Young Pastor's Network." If I were accepted, I would receive an invitation to be part of this mentoring program hosted by Adam Hamilton and Mike Slaughter—senior pastors of two of the largest United Methodist churches in America at that time.

This was incredible! He explained that this was a two-year program of being directly mentored by Adam and Mike while visiting and learning at their two churches in Kansas and Ohio—United Methodist Church of the Resurrection and Ginghamsburg Church, respectively. Only around forty people who show the most promise for leading large United Methodist churches are accepted into this amazing opportunity every few years.

I was over the moon! I couldn't say yes fast enough. This was a networking opportunity of a lifetime that would connect me with these two ultra-talented, prominent pastors and connect me with forty of the brightest rising stars in the United Methodist Church. I thought this opportunity would fast-track my career and help set me up for life. What an exclusive group to be invited into!

This should help me get an appointment as a senior pastor quickly. I'd have a huge United Methodist congregation of my own in no time, I thought. Sometimes, I forget the power of an invitation and the importance of networking. Networking equals net-worthing, right? Strengthening my network means strengthening my net worth, income, and opportunities to move up in the world. Those are the kind of invitations that really get your attention. Networking is a major focus of almost every business training I have ever attended. It involves building relationships and spending time with those who can help you advance in your career.

Jesus had received one of those coveted, exclusive invitations when you meet him in today's story from Luke 14. Jesus graciously accepts the invitation to a fancy dinner at the house of a Pharisee, even though Jesus sometimes butts heads and has an occasional argument with some of the Pharisees who are a little too partisan, a little too judgmental, and a little too exclusive.

Once he arrives, Jesus sits back and watches the hullabaloo. This is a big feast for the social elite, and they all seem to be jockeying and jostling for position. As the guests arrive, folks scramble to grab a seat in the VIP section near the host in a place of prominence, trying to fast-track their advancement and status in the world. Jesus watches the guests continue to structure and perfect their exclusive snobby bubbles—the bubbles they've spent a lifetime constructing—separating who is in and who is out, who is worthy and who is unworthy.

I don't know about you, but I don't like it when Jesus points out how I have more in common with these Pharisees than I like to think or admit. Unfortunately, I see too much of myself in them; I have a finely curated bubble. My Facebook feed no longer shows me posts from folks I disagree with because I have clicked the "unfollow" button anytime I see a post I did not like. I love to stay at all-inclusive resorts on vacation because I don't have to worry about running into the riffraff. It appears that I have gotten some things wrong and have some tendencies that need re-evaluating. Jesus doesn't seem to be much of a fan of these exclusive bubbles. He seems to prefer inclusion over exclusion.

From day one, *Mister Rogers' Neighborhood* was a radically inclusive kids' television show. This show faced discrimination and divisions in a way that only Mr. Rogers could. Fred Rogers is probably the best example I have seen from my childhood of inclusively loving your neighbor. Rogers genuinely meant it when he said, "Won't you be my neighbor?"

From Latrobe, Pennsylvania, Fred Rogers was a music major who was all set to go to seminary after college.[8] He came home for summer break, saw his parents' brand-new TV for the first time, and witnessed slapstick comedy with people throwing pies at each other's faces for a laugh. He thought, "This is a wonderful tool. Why is it being used so badly?"

This feeling stuck with Rogers, and after he graduated from seminary, he knew that even television was a place where one should love one's neighbor as oneself. So he decided to do something about it. Fred Rogers was ordained by the Presbyterian Church as an evangelist to children through the platform of television.

This ordained minister armed himself with a cardigan, blue boat shoes, and some puppets and went into battle every week, broadcasting grace throughout the land for half an hour a day, five days a week. This minister never really wrote a sermon, but he preached

---

[8] Morgan Neville, dir., *Won't You Be My Neighbor?* (Tremolo Productions, 2018), Documentary Film.

the gospel every week, especially how to love your neighbor as yourself.

Did you know that Fred Rogers' favorite number was 143—1. 4. 3. "I" has one letter. "Love" has four letters. And "You" has three letters—143. Every day after his morning devotion and prayer time, from the late 1950s until he died fifty years later, Fred Rogers swam a mile and then got on the scale and watched the needle jump to 143 pounds. He weighed 143 pounds for fifty-plus years!

Each morning, when he read 143 on the scale, it was another message telling him, "I love you." Weighing 143 pounds every day for fifty years reminded him to tell himself, "I love you," which then helped him go out and more fully love his neighbor each and every day. Rogers stated, "Love is at the root of everything—all learning, all parenting, all relationships—love, or the lack of it."[9] "Everyone longs to be loved and wants to know that he or she is lovable." Rogers showed us that one of the greatest things we can do to love our neighbor is to help somebody know they are loved and capable of loving.

A Hells Angel taught me how to say "I love you" and mean it! It's true. He was known as "Crazy Carl." (Though he never said outright that the Hells Angels was the motorcycle gang he rode with, all the hints pointed in that direction.) His arms were covered in tattoos full of nudity

---

[9] *Mr. Rogers' Neighborhood,* episode 1065, Fred Rogers, writer, Chen, David Fu-Ying, dir., aired May 9, 1969, on WQED.

and violent imagery. Carl smoked, cursed, and rode around on Harley-Davidson motorcycles. He usually had a long, scruffy beard and a unibrow.

Carl was one of my scout leaders in the Boy Scouts of America as a youth. I am pretty sure that, by today's standards of youth protection, there is a strong possibility that Carl would not pass the criminal background checks to be a scout leader now. But that was a different time. Carl was a crass, gritty, coarse, and earthy kind of guy. He always wore boots and a leather motorcycle jacket, and his wallet had a chain connecting to his belt. Carl was salty! It wasn't until deeper in my adulthood that I could see being salty as a strength instead of a character flaw.

Crazy Carl was about the nittiest-grittiest person I have ever known. As my scout leader, he taught me many skills, such as how to believe in myself and the characteristics that make a good leader. He also shared tidbits of wisdom like "Remember that no matter where you go … there you are." But he was also a truly authentic human being.

As we shared life together, he would open up about his life's stories with me. Born in San Francisco in 1949, he was drafted and fought in the Vietnam War. Once he made it home, he struggled with post-traumatic stress disorder (PTSD) and drug addiction, which led to a time of homelessness like so many other of our veterans. He went on to ride with the Hells Angels, which included all the drugs and violence you could imagine going along with it.

As he got older, Crazy Carl found family, faith, and healing. He dedicated his life to mentoring young men. He was the first person outside my immediate family to tell me "I love you." And he said it every time he saw me. And he said it to everyone he knew every time he saw them. But he said it in his own Crazy Carl way: "I love you, man!" as his tattooed arms wrapped around me and his long beard tickled my ears.

Carl was open and honest with me about his struggles with PTSD, homelessness, and drugs. He did not hide that he was once part of a motorcycle gang. His salty authenticity and vulnerability showed me the amazing nitty-gritty, salty side of God. Maybe this is what Jesus meant when he told his followers to be the "salt of the earth" (Matthew 5:13).

Despite his past struggles, Carl was one of the most gifted mentors of young people I have ever encountered. Just as Carl's history didn't define him, he was that accepting of others. Whether someone had Down syndrome, had parents who were doctors, or came from a broken home, I saw each young man reach Eagle Scout under Crazy Carl's guidance.

Crazy Carl's salty personality was a testament that taught me that your past or present predicaments do not define who you are to God, and they should not define who you are to each other. You find your identity in community when you are painfully and awkwardly transparent and authentic before God and each other.

It was heart-wrenching to see Crazy Carl lose his battle with a type of brain cancer called glioblastoma. But at his funeral, I found so much hope in a roomful of grown men who had found meaning and purpose through Crazy Carl's presence in their lives. From tattoo artists to doctors, meteorologists to geophysicists, and even to this preacher, that room showed me that this world is a better place because of Crazy Carl. Carl was the opposite of Mr. Rogers in almost every way except that he helped teach me and many others what it looks like to live out God's radical, vulnerable, and inclusive love that breaks the rules and boundaries.

My favorite example of Fred Rogers beautifully breaking boundaries happened in 1969 when an episode of Mister Rogers' Neighborhood broke the color barrier. Though segregation was no longer the law of the land by the end of the 1960s, Black citizens were still not embraced as equal participants in public life. This was the case at many community pools where Blacks were not allowed to swim with Whites. In this atmosphere, Fred Rogers performed a simple but meaningful act between Mister Rogers and Officer Clemmons in "Episode 1065" of Mister Rogers' Neighborhood, which aired on May 9, 1969. Police Officer Clemmons was played by François Clemmons, an African American.

This show was already pretty radically welcoming because police officers in the late '60s were not known for being people of color. They were more often known for abusing people of color with high-powered water hoses and police dogs, so being a show with a police officer of color, Mister Rogers' Neighborhood was already making a huge statement of invitation, welcome, and inclusion.

The most powerful example of this happened with a silly little kiddie pool. On one hot summer day, the show featured Mr. Rogers sitting in a lawn chair with his pants rolled up, barefooted, soaking his feet in the cool water of a kiddie pool. Officer Clemmons of the neighborhood police walked by, and Mr. Rogers invited him to sit in the other lawn chair and cool his feet in the refreshing kiddie pool. The sweet moment of Mr. Rogers and Officer Clemmons sitting in lawn chairs side-by-side with their pants rolled up and their feet in the pool was Fred Rogers' tender and compassionate way to speak out against a practice where society was failing to fully love its neighbor. When Clemmons accepted this invitation, sat down, and placed his feet in the water right next to Rogers, the two men broke a well-known color barrier—then they even shared a towel.

Wow! Who knew such a powerful moment could happen on a little kids' television show? Powerful moments can happen just about anywhere! Jesus tells you it's up to you to make them happen. It often just takes a little courage and an invitation—courage to step out of your comfy, safe protective bubble and give an invitation to your neighbor.

But not those neighbors you always hang out with. It is not about blessing the blessed. Jesus says it's time you start inviting your poor neighbor, your oppressed and depressed neighbor, your excluded neighbor. Fred Rogers said, "Won't you be my neighbor?" is an invitation. "It's an invitation for somebody to be close to you, to live in relationship."[10]

It is easy to underestimate the power of an invitation. This faith journey is about relationship. An invitation has the power to change lives—of the invitee and the inviter. It is time you start giving out some invites. Eight out of ten people visit a church because of an invitation from a friend or coworker. "Won't you be a neighbor?"

This is your homework. Offer an invitation—to come to church, go out for lunch, talk, or see a movie. Bless someone who can give you nothing in return. It just might change their life—and yours. "Could you be mine? Would you be mine? Won't you be a neighbor?"

---

[10] Morgan Neville, dir., *Won't You Be My Neighbor?*

Reflection Questions:

Have you ever received a life-changing invitation? If so, how did it impact your life?

When you consider your own life, do you have any Crazy Carls who were surprising examples of grace?

What barriers do you feel that Jesus is inviting you to break through? What's the first step you can take right away?

Who are "the poor, the crippled, the blind, and the lame" in your community that need to be invited to the feast? Maybe you will not use a kiddie pool, but what are some ways you can break down these barriers of exclusion and injustice?

Prayer:

O God, I pray that you can use me to live out your good news to love my neighbor as myself. Show me the poor, the crippled, the blind, and the lame in my community that need to be invited to the feast. Give me courage to offer an invitation or accept an invitation. Give me the strength to include the excluded. Give me the heart to love all your children. In your name, I offer this prayer. Amen!

Lesson 3

God Designed Diversity
Lesson by Michelle Morris

About the Lesson Writer:

Rev. Dr. Michelle Morris has served Arkansas churches in West Memphis, Fort Smith, and Conway and is now the lead pastor at First United Methodist Church in Bentonville, Arkansas. She also worked for the Center for Vitality in the Conference offices, helping to transition churches to online ministry during the outbreak of the pandemic. She writes for the *Adult Bible Studies Curriculum* and is the author of *Gospel Discipleship: Four Pathways for Christian Disciples.*

Scripture Lesson
Genesis 11:1-9, Acts 2:1-11

> *All people on the earth had one language and the same words. When they traveled east, they found a valley in the land of Shinar and settled there. They said to each other, "Come, let's make bricks and bake them hard." They used bricks for stones and asphalt for mortar. They said, "Come, let's build for ourselves a city and a tower with its top in the sky, and let's make a name for ourselves so that we won't be dispersed over all the earth."*

> *Then the Lord came down to see the city and the tower that the humans built. And the Lord said, "There is now one people and they all have one language. This is what they have begun to do, and now all that they plan to do will be possible for them. Come, let's go down and mix*

up their language there so they won't understand each other's language." Then the Lord dispersed them from there over all of the earth, and they stopped building the city. Therefore, it is named Babel, because there the Lord mixed up the language of all the earth; and from there the Lord dispersed them over all the earth.

Genesis 11:1-9 (CEB)

When Pentecost Day arrived, they were all together in one place. Suddenly a sound from heaven like the howling of a fierce wind filled the entire house where they were sitting. They saw what seemed to be individual flames of fire alighting on each one of them. They were all filled with the Holy Spirit and began to speak in other languages as the Spirit enabled them to speak.

There were pious Jews from every nation under heaven living in Jerusalem. When they heard this sound, a crowd gathered. They were mystified because everyone heard them speaking in their native languages. They were surprised and amazed, saying, "Look, aren't all the people who are speaking Galileans, every one of them? How then can each of us hear them speaking in our native language? Parthians, Medes, and Elamites; as well as residents of Mesopotamia, Judea, and Cappadocia, Pontus and Asia, Phrygia and Pamphylia, Egypt and the regions of Libya bordering Cyrene; and visitors from Rome (both Jews and converts to Judaism), Cretans and Arabs—we hear them declaring the mighty works of God in our own languages!"

Acts 2:1-11 (CEB)

There's a Book Named Zephaniah in the Bible?

Last year, my congregation was challenged to read the Bible cover-to-cover. For many, it was their first time undertaking this endeavor. Even lifelong Christians had never done it. To support us all in the journey, I preached from at least one of the passages we read for the week, and I offered two opportunities for extra study where anyone could drop in, ask questions, or share any revelations they had experienced.

The journey was incredibly rewarding, made all the more so because we went on it together. There were three experiences, however, that kept coming up over and over. The first was alluded to in the exclamation that opened this lesson: people were regularly surprised by all the things in the Bible that they did not know existed. Some surprises admittedly were better than others; I had a whole crew of people who were angry about pretty much the entire book of Judges. The second experience primarily occurred as we read through the Gospels. It was the first time people treated each Gospel as telling a continuous story. We are accustomed to hearing the Gospels (really all of scripture) chunked up into small passages, so people don't see how one story flows into the next and the next. It changed understandings of many of the passages we all thought we knew so well.

The final experience is the one we will explore today: people noticed connections between passages that were far apart in their locations in the Bible and in the time and place written. I love it when people have that kind of experience. First, it helps us stop talking about the Old and New Testaments as if they are isolated from one another (and especially helps us quit thinking that the New Testament is better). But it also helps us understand the continuity of God's story, how it unfolds throughout the Bible, and how it carries on in our lives as well. It pulls us all together, connected by one common thread of narrative: a narrative of becoming the people of God.

Finding connections across the narrative can profoundly impact how we understand our faith. I had just such an experience when I was in seminary and read an article by Bernhard Anderson.[11] He was analyzing the Tower of Babel story, particularly the reason God would object to the tower. We tend to read that story and think the problem God has is that we are trying to be like God. We get that from Genesis 11:6 where God says, "Now all that they plan to do will be possible for them." But Anderson points out that is not what disturbs God as God takes notice. What disturbs God is this: "There is now one people and they all have one language."

Now, wait a minute, what is wrong with that? Doesn't that seem like a good thing? We could all live together, and we could all understand each other, and we could all work together! Doesn't that seem like a utopia? Maybe. But first, let's note what we do when we all get together. We build a tower. What do you need a tower for? Defense. We took a stance of fear, even though theoretically, we

---

[11] Bernhard T. Anderson, "Unity and Diversity in God's Creation: A Study of the Babel Story," *From Creation to New Creation: Biblical Theology and Exegesis*, eds. Daniel M. Gurtner and Benjamin L. Gladd (Hendrickson Academic, 2013).

should all be safe! We are all together as one. What do we need a tower for? And what do we need a name for? To inspire fear—in whom? In the choices we make when we are one, we give away that we are still preparing for battle, and we are still reacting out of fear.

But Anderson also points out something key to this story. We are disobeying the very first commandment God gave humanity. Now remember, this is before the Ten Commandments are given. That will be years and years down the road in the narrative. No, for the first commandment given to humanity, we must turn to the very first chapter in the very first book of the Bible: "God blessed them and said to them, 'Be fertile and multiply; fill the earth and master it'" (Genesis 1:28a). When we chose to huddle together, to be one people with one language, we were disobeying God's wishes for us. We were not filling the earth, and we were not multiplying. We were scrunching together and ignoring the plan for diversity that God had invited us into. Multiplying is not simply about being more in number. It is also about being all kinds of people, with all kinds of ways of life and all kinds of understandings. So when we refused God's dream for us, God gave us a nudge. A scattering nudge.

That was not the last time God nudged us. For another example, let's now jump ahead to another defining moment in the narrative of God's people, the birth of the church: Pentecost.

Here we find another group of people huddled together. They have put themselves in an upper room (see Acts 1:13), a tower of sorts, probably so they have a good vantage point to see those they consider their enemies, the ones who have made them afraid. They are indeed under threat but have also been entrusted with the world's most important message. And just as God instructed the human race to fill all the earth, Jesus has charged these people with the instructions that they "will be my witnesses in Jerusalem, in all Judea and Samaria, and to the end of the earth" (Acts 1:8b). And here God's people are again, defying the very instructions they have been given (though arguably they are still waiting on the Holy Spirit, so we can cut them some slack, I suppose).

And then here comes the nudge: a fierce wind and tongues of fire. Suddenly, people from all over the world are hearing God's gospel shared in their own languages. Now this small group of people, who used to be holed up in an upper room and who all spoke the same language, are set loose and empowered to take this story anywhere and everywhere it needs to be heard and to do so in ways that are meaningful to the diverse people they encounter. They will multiply the means of salvation and fill all the earth with God's Good News!

Notably, they were empowered to tell the story in *different* languages to people of *different* cultures. Actually, we do not know if the disciples could speak different languages or if the people could hear in their own language, or both. The text is ambiguous. We do know, however, that God did not force everyone into one common language. The dream God has for us continues. God does not want us to all speak the same. God does not want us to have one way of understanding. God may have a story God wants all of us to share, but God wants that sharing to take place in a variety of tongues and perspectives. The birth of the church is a rebirth of that design God sought for us from the very beginning. Multiply. And fill all the earth.

Have you ever experienced the joy of our diversity? Have you ever encountered someone whose way of life was so different from yours, and yet, as you shared, you realized what a blessing it is to see the world from their perspective? I used to work as a study-abroad advisor for the University of Arkansas, which meant I worked with both American students and exchange students from around the world. I also have studied five languages other than English, and my study of French led me to spend a summer in France. Some of the most transformative moments I have experienced have come from my encounters with people who live and speak differently than I do.

For instance, as part of my study-abroad work, I was sent to Denmark to learn about one of our partner programs, and I stayed with a host mother. She had to leave early for work, earlier than I had to be downtown the next day, so she showed me where the bread, meat, and toaster were so I could make toast for breakfast and a sandwich to take with me for lunch. However, she did not show me how to slice bread (I had been raised solely on pre-sliced bread loaves up to that point). I made an utter mess of the bread loaf, but I managed to get enough bread to pack around some meat and then one kind of slice to make toast. But then I spent fifteen minutes trying to figure out how to actually get the toaster to work. It was unplugged. Again, I had never had the experience of unplugging appliances that lived on the counter. Suddenly, I had a very real understanding of how much passive electricity we consume in our country and how automated so much of our lives are compared to the rest of the world. As a result, I could not make toast. I felt like the punchline to a bad joke. It was both a humbling and enlightening experience.

Or how about when I learned that people in Iceland celebrate Jolabokaflod—Christmas book flood—on Christmas Day? They exchange books for Christmas and then spend the day reading and eating chocolate. For a pastor who lives alone and is usually completely wiped out on Christmas Day after the intensity of Christmas Eve, this holiday is a gift from heaven. Because I know I am not truly alone in celebrating it either (a whole country is participating with me), it gives a warmth to the day that has been absent since I found myself alone. I am grateful for this different way of celebrating

Christmas, a way that includes people like me.

Studying another language also helped me understand the limits of my own language in expressing the fullness of the human condition. Did you know that the Germans have a word, Kummerspeck, that literally means "grief bacon," but that connotes the weight you gain from depression? I don't know about you, but I need this word in my life! Also, I once had a somewhat embarrassing-but-revelatory moment when someone asked me how to say, "I'm glad to meet you" in French. I had just told the person I had studied French for seven years, but I stood there dumbfounded and had no answer to their question. "Never mind," the frustrated person said and then walked away. Just a few seconds later, I realized why I couldn't think of the answer. There is no word for "glad" in French; it is way too wimpy of an emotion. Enchanté—that's what the French say when they meet you. They are enchanted to meet you, not just glad!

At the heart of all these experiences, though, is one nagging question, raised at least in part by the misunderstandings that kept occurring: why would God want diversity? The first response is to affirm that it is impossible as a human to know exactly why God wants anything. If we stopped there, though, then there really would be no point to our faith at all. Seeking to follow God is a lifelong journey of trying to understand what God really wants of us. Part of how we make that journey is in the study of scripture, and today, we have seen through scripture that God gets somewhat insistent about our differences, enough to scatter us to create difference and then to empower us in that difference. So asking why God wants diversity is definitely a fair question.

Before we address why God wants diversity, can we take a moment to discuss what a problem diversity is for us? All our different ways of being create vast misunderstandings among us. Those misunderstandings result in division. Sometimes that division rises to anger. Sometimes that anger escalates to war. Why would God want us to be at war?

I think that is a false narrative, however. That division and hate is a result of our sin. If you ask me for a definition of sin, I will say it is a broken relationship between us and God and between us and each other—and again, I return to Genesis for that definition. When the man and the woman made choices that divided them from God and each other, sin crept into the world and then was birthed in its fullness when one of their sons murdered the other one (the very first mention of sin is in the Cain and Abel story in Genesis 4:7).

Additionally, the nature of war is to seek to eliminate the diversity among us. Recall the films you have seen of Hitler's Nazis goose-stepping down German streets. They are all in identical uniforms, all in the same lockstep, all performing the same movements. It is during war that opposing viewpoints are often discouraged or punished. Propaganda moves us to think the same, act the same, and believe the same. War is an engine that defies diversity. War consists of those same fears within us that drive us to gather together, build a tower, and prop up our own names so we might be the most powerful, the most feared, and the least diverse.

And now we have one reason that God desires diversity. Hopefully, we do not fall prey to group-think when we gather. Hopefully, there are enough of us with different perspectives and life experiences that when a dangerous or deceptive word comes along, someone says, "Wait a minute, this does not seem like a good idea!" Hopefully, dissension leads to discernment in the healthiest situations and helps us all do better.

There are at least two other reasons, however, that God cares enough about diversity to urge it along. Diversity creates the fertile field on which we practice loving our neighbor. It is far too easy to love someone who is exactly like me. That kind of love is selfish—do I truly love that person, or do I really just love myself? Coming into contact with someone who is unlike me, in whatever ways, allows me to truly practice generous and gracious love. That practice of love also grows and changes me. It broadens my perspective and trains me to love even more fully as I encounter all the interesting people in life. And the same is true for you. It is true for all of us.

Our perspective, then, is not just expanded regarding how we understand and love people. It also expands our understanding and love of God. I turn one more time to the opening of Genesis, the passage just before our first commandment: "God created humanity in God's own image, in the divine image God created them, male and female God created them" (Genesis 1:27). All of humanity is created in God's image. Individually, yes, but also collectively. Each of us has a piece of that image of God, but collectively, we can see God's fuller image. It is as if there is one giant God puzzle, and we are pieces of it.

Our interaction with others helps us expand our understanding of God. God is so much bigger than just one person. When I insulate myself from people, particularly those who are different than me, my theology also suffers. Worse than that, God begins to look more and more like me. When I am worshiping a God who looks just like me, then I am really worshiping myself, and that, my friends, is idolatry.

We need diversity, then, to truly love each other and to truly love God. The Greatest Commandments depend on difference. In a world that is increasingly trying to push us into tribalism and division, we are called to let love push past those boundaries. We should not seek to erase difference but to celebrate it, empower it, and learn from it. And above all else, we should let such diversity lead us into fuller understanding and deeper love.

Reflection Questions:

When have you ever felt like a fish out of water? Did you always feel that way in that situation, or did someone help you feel like you belonged? If someone helped you feel like you belonged, how did they do that?

Think of a time you had an opportunity to get to know someone who has lived a very different life than you have. What did you learn from that person? How has that interaction shaped your life going forward?

If you have studied the Bible in a group setting with people who see scripture differently, or if you have read a Bible lesson that approaches a passage differently than you have, how has that helped you grow in your faith?

Sometimes we clash with others, creating a division between us that is too deep for us to overcome. In those cases, what difference does our relationship with God make? How can or how has God provided a space of healing?

How is God different for you now than earlier in your faith journey? What has contributed to that difference?

What is the difference between unity and uniformity? Which do you think God seeks in us, and why?

Lesson 4

Reaching the Least, Last, and Lost
Lesson by Dan Read

About the Lesson Writer:

Dan Read received his Master's of Divinity from Duke Divinity School in 2016, and he now serves the Arkansas Annual Conference as an ordained elder. Dan is also the chair of the Arkansas Committee on Native American Ministry and is an enrolled member of the Choctaw Nation of Oklahoma.

Scripture Lesson:
Luke 15:11-32

Jesus continued: "There was a man who had two sons. The younger one said to his father, 'Father, give me my share of the estate.' So he divided his property between them. "Not long after that, the younger son got together all he had, set off for a distant country and there squandered his wealth in wild living. After he had spent everything, there was a severe famine in that whole country, and he began to be in need. So he went and hired himself out to a citizen of that country, who sent him to his fields to feed pigs. He longed to fill his stomach with the pods that the pigs were eating, but no one gave him anything.

"When he came to his senses, he said, 'How many of my father's hired servants have food to spare, and here I am starving to death! I will set out and go back to my father and say to him: Father, I have sinned against heaven and

against you. I am no longer worthy to be called your son; make me like one of your hired servants.' So he got up and went to his father. "But while he was still a long way off, his father saw him and was filled with compassion for him; he ran to his son, threw his arms around him and kissed him. "The son said to him, 'Father, I have sinned against heaven and against you. I am no longer worthy to be called your son.' "But the father said to his servants, 'Quick! Bring the best robe and put it on him. Put a ring on his finger and sandals on his feet. Bring the fattened calf and kill it. Let's have a feast and celebrate. For this son of mine was dead and is alive again; he was lost and is found.' So they began to celebrate."

"Meanwhile, the older son was in the field. When he came near the house, he heard music and dancing. So he called one of the servants and asked him what was going on. 'Your brother has come,' he replied, 'and your father has killed the fattened calf because he has him back safe and sound.'

"The older brother became angry and refused to go in. So his father went out and pleaded with him. But he answered his father, 'Look! All these years I've been slaving for you and never disobeyed your orders. Yet you never gave me even a young goat so I could celebrate with my friends. But when this son of yours who has squandered your property with prostitutes comes home, you kill the fattened calf for him!'

"'My son,' the father said, 'you are always with me, and everything I have is yours. But we had to celebrate and be glad, because this brother of yours was dead and is alive again; he was lost and is found.'"

Luke 15:11-32 (NIV)

Let's take an in-depth look at the parable of the prodigal son. One reason for such an in-depth look at this particular parable is that it only appears here in Chapter 15 of the Gospel of Luke. It is in none of the other Gospels and is emblematic of some themes throughout the Gospel of Luke. One central theme intertwined in Luke's Gospel is the special attention Jesus shows toward the least, the last, and the lost.

First, examine the context of the parable of the prodigal. This story directly follows the parable of the lost sheep and the parable of the lost coin. How do these parables, and in particular the parable of the prodigal, fit into Luke's theme of reaching the least, the last, and the lost?

To answer this question, we should first read Luke 15:1-2: "Now all the tax-collectors and sinners were coming near to listen to him. And the Pharisees and the scribes were grumbling and saying, 'This fellow welcomes sinners and eats with them'" (NRSV).

All kinds of people find their way to Jesus for a variety of reasons. His disciples want to learn from him, the sick want to be healed, and the religious leaders want to spy on him. The sinners and outcasts don't fit with any particular group, so Jesus seeks them out. Jesus directly addresses those present and the charges that he eats with sinners in these parables. By welcoming and eating with sinners, Jesus is identifying himself: he's a Jewish rabbi with sinners. Jesus is claiming them as his people, and this is unacceptable to the Pharisees and scribes witnessing his ministry. Why might Jesus be speaking to his audience in the form of parables?

As you read through the story of the prodigal,

identify the different characters and what Jesus might be saying about God, sinners, and the religious through the use of those characters. In Chapter 15, verses 11 through 12, Jesus presents a father with two sons. The younger son requests his inheritance. This request would have been a tremendous insult because the younger son's father was still alive. What does this tell us initially about the character of the younger son? What does it tell us about the character of the father who granted the younger son's request?

Look first at the story of the younger son. Read verses 13-19. The younger son goes away and squanders all he has been given. When a famine hits the land, the younger son must resort to pig farming. For Jews, pigs were the image of uncleanliness, an abomination before the Lord, and to be a pig farmer was to be cursed. Why do you think Jesus chose that job for the younger son? How might those listening to Jesus respond to such an outrageous job? The young man is broke and starving. Wallowing in the muck of a pig pen, he has hit rock bottom. When we hit rock bottom and have nothing left, we often turn to our heavenly father. We now learn that the younger son comes up with a plan. He plans to return to his father and be treated like one of his hired servants now that he has lost everything he once had. We also learn that the father treats his servants like family, ensuring they do not go hungry. As you enter the story as the younger son, think about these questions:

Have you ever felt like you have ruined everything and wish you could take it all back? How did you bargain with God to be forgiven? Was your bargaining like that of the prodigal son?

Focus now on the love of the father. Read verses 20-24. Here, we learn of a father's great compassion. Before the son can say anything, the father runs to him. In fact, the father ignores the son when he speaks and orders that his best robe and family ring be brought. Why might this have been done? It is likely that the son's clothes were tattered and smelly and that he was not in the best health. The father wanted to cover his son's shame and restore his authority by giving him their family ring. Jesus uses powerful imagery in the story of the prodigal, so much so that you can visualize and almost feel the embrace between father and son as they are reunited. In the parables of the lost, Jesus tells us that our heavenly father is always ready to welcome us with open arms and that our God is a God who seeks the lost and does not stop until God finds all who have been misplaced and mishandled.

Our celebratory story about a long-lost son returning home takes a dark turn. Now we are confronted with an ill-tempered and entitled elder brother. Let us not forget that he would still get the double portion of his inheritance, which he did not earn but was his birthright simply for being the firstborn son. The parable does not end with the embrace between father and son like we want. Instead, as we read verses 25-31, the elder son enters the story again. He is upset that his brother is being welcomed back and not getting what he thinks he deserves. The older brother is so angry that he refuses to join the party despite the father's pleading. Dynamics between siblings often create rivalries. If you have a brother or sister, you know what this feels like. There most certainly was a rivalry between the two brothers in our Gospel lesson today. From the onset, it appears the two brothers could not be more different from each other. They saw the world very differently, and because of that, they acted very differently from one another. The younger brother was arrogant, asking for his share of the inheritance early. We also learn that he was incredibly foolish, wasting all he had been given, and we learned that he returned to his father asking for forgiveness and finding grace beyond measure. It appears the elder brother thinks very highly of himself. After all, he claims he has worked diligently for years, never asking for anything, never disobeying, and never leaving.

It is clear that the elder brother becomes jealous and resentful of his brother:

> "Listen! For all these years I have been working like a slave for you, and I have never disobeyed your command; yet you have never given me even a young goat so that I might celebrate with my friends. But when this son of yours came back, who has devoured your property with prostitutes, you killed the fatted calf for him!"

Did you hear that? The older brother calls his brother, "This son of yours." If we are to take him at his word, then he should be pitied. He is the poor older brother who did everything right and got nothing in return. But there are always two sides to the story. He has removed himself from his familial relation, and now his brother is his father's problem. Have you ever been angry when someone else did not receive the punishment you thought they should?

I started my faith journey as an elder brother. As a teen, I felt I had all the right doctrinal beliefs. I knew who was in and who was out of God's kingdom, which groups of people were going to hell and which were not. I knew who my brothers were and who were not worthy of being called brothers and sisters in Christ, and I could quote proof texts from scripture to prove it! Like so many lost in a legalistic faith, I thought I was serving God. However, my heart was far from God and those loved by God. Just like the elder brother, I could not see the pain and suffering of those around me because I was too busy being self-righteous. My faith was not in the person of Jesus Christ but in the infallibility of my interpretation of the Bible. It took the love and grace of God to break my heart. Our life and walk with God are a continuous struggle to not walk away like the prodigal son and to not turn into the resentful and judgmental elder brother. We must be on the lookout and constantly vigilant before becoming complacent, falling into one struggle over another.

I have always loved how artists interpret and create out of the stories of scripture. One of my favorite sculptures is a depiction in bronze of the parable of the prodigal titled "Reconciliation" by Margaret Adams Parker, located in a courtyard at Duke Divinity School. While attending Duke Divinity, I passed the sculpture daily, and it always left an impact: the prodigal clinging to his father, the father reaching out to the older brother, and the older brother turning away with arms crossed. It depicts the father's longing to embrace both sons and the older brother's inability to look at his father or brother. This sculpture physically depicts the image I always imagine when reading the story of the prodigal from scripture. You can feel the father's longing for both of his sons as well as the older brother's stubborn resentment in his crossed arms and turned face.

The story of the prodigal son is emblematic of the themes in the Gospel of Luke and the central message of redemption in the gospel of Jesus Christ. Jesus uses this parable to teach the sinners and tax collectors who were present that God is like a loving father who will forgive them when they return to him. It is also clear that Jesus does not take kindly to the religiously judgmental whose own stubbornness keeps them from the kingdom of God. Jesus, through the story of the prodigal, is bringing all kinds of people into the kingdom of God and begins to form a new community of believers. People who were lost and who have now been found. The sinners, foreigners, tax collectors, and prostitutes.

The religious leaders and the scribes have always had God with them, but now is the time to celebrate that the lost are returning home. This concept is unacceptable for the religious elite in Israel. They know that those people are not their people. After all, those people are unclean; those people need to be punished; they are sinners. One of the hardest things in the world is to stop being the prodigal son without turning into the elder brother. When we return to God and feel we have finally gotten our lives together, we are most susceptible to becoming the elder brother. The parable challenges the reader to ask who truly are the last, least, and lost in the kingdom of God.

Reflection Questions:

Why does Jesus teach in parables?

Who do you relate to most in the parable, and have you always felt this way?

How might both brothers feel lost?

Lesson 5

Love Abiding
A Commentary on the Fifteenth Chapter of John
Lesson by Michael Roberts

About the Lesson Writer:

Michael Roberts currently serves as senior pastor of First United Methodist Church in Jonesboro, Arkansas, and previously served in the same position at First United Methodist Church in Conway, Arkansas.

Scripture Lesson:
John 15:4, 15:9

> *Abide in me as I abide in you. Just as the branch cannot bear fruit by itself unless it abides in the vine, neither can you unless you abide in me.*
>
> **John 15:4 (NRSV)**

> *As the Father has loved me, so I have loved you; abide in my love.*
>
> **John 15:9 (NRSV)**

An Approachable God

When I was a child, I was sure God had white hair, a deep, booming male voice, and spoke with an accent. God didn't talk like me. God said, "I command you," and drew out his name, making God into a multi-syllable word: Gawd. This image did not surface from my own imagination. It had deep roots in the culture. The image was reinforced in art, sermons, and incarnate examples of pastors who stood before us on Sunday mornings. There were not many other models. The pastors I knew in my early years all fit this image to some degree and tended to speak for GAWD with great authority.

My wife tells a story of how one particular pastor came to her church and rocked her theological world. As older children, they were gathered in the fellowship hall. They all brought pillows and blankets and scattered on the floor to watch a movie. She can still see the scene and hear the clicks of the projector, which today would be a novelty. This pastor came in and plopped down in the middle of this group of children. She remembers the pastor stuffing popcorn in his mouth and laughing, and her first thought was, "He can't do that." GAWD doesn't act that way.

I had a similar experience when we moved and went to a new church. The pastor was approachable in a way that I had not experienced before. He, too, would sit down with us, with legs crossed on the floor, and engage in conversation. He would tell stories and try to be funny. I remember this rocking my theological world as well. This pastor knew me by name and his genuine care for me opened the way to a new understanding of faith.

In a loose translation, that is what John says God did in Jesus Christ when "the Word became flesh and dwelt among us" (John 1:14). God plopped God's self in our midst and made a home. The word translated as "dwelt" in the first chapter of John is a synonym of the word Jesus used later when he said, "Abide in me as I abide in you" (John 15:4). These two words combine to open us to a new understanding of God.

Making a Home

In Greek, the word translated as "dwell" (skenoo) means to "set up a tent." It is related to the Hebrew word for "tabernacle," which was a sanctuary that moved with the people and provided a place for God to dwell among them.

The word most often translated as "abide" (meno) is the root word for "home" or "dwelling place." In John 14, the word is translated as "mansions," where Jesus says there are many dwelling places or mansions in the Father's home, and he would go and prepare a place for us. The message is that we will abide with him in heaven, even as he abides with us and in us in this present season.

Abide! It means to make a home. It connotes something more permanent than a tent. It calls for faithfulness and fidelity. To abide is to "be there" through thick and thin, to make a commitment. To abide is to be loyal and steadfast. It is a call to remain, to be present and attentive. Abide! It is not a call to merely visit but to make a home. Jesus is inviting us to bring our pillows and make ourselves at home in the holy, even as God makes a home in us and with us.

I didn't quite grasp all this as a child. All I knew was that something moved in me as I made room for a representative of God to plop down in the middle of our gathering to talk and laugh. I remember thinking about this at the time. Maybe God was not so fearsome and unapproachable after all. Maybe God wanted to get to know me as much as I wanted to know God. Or maybe—even better—God did know me and wanted to be in my presence. I am so thankful for this witness, which continues to come through many siblings within the body of Christ, clergy and lay, female and male, and all through whom love shines.

It is worth noting that Jesus gives this witness to friends. We read, "I no longer call you servants, because the servant does not know what the master is doing, but I have called you friends, because I have made known to you everything that I have heard from my Father" (John 15:15, CSB). There is an intimacy in this holy abiding.

The Rhythm of Love

And where does this lead? Immediately after Jesus speaks of abiding, he gives a version of the great commandment. He says, "This is my commandment, that you love one another as I have loved you" (John 15:12, NRSV). This commandment is set up with the phrase "abide in my love," repeated twice in the preceding verses, along with a comparison to how Christ abides in God's love. We read:

> *As the Father has loved me, so I have loved you; abide in my love. If you keep my commandments, you will abide in my love, just as I have kept my Father's commandments and abide in his love.*
>
> **John 15:9-10, NRSV**

If a phrase is repeated, it is important. Jesus wants to make the connection clear. Love is the key to making a good home; it is also the fruit that comes from it.

Notice the similarities in phrasing here: "Abide in me as I abide in you," "Love one another as I have loved you," and "As the Father has loved me, so I have loved you." I invite you to breathe these words in and out and experience the holy rhythm. As another exercise, I invite you to say these phrases aloud with hand motions from above to the heart and then outward to the world. God's love comes to us on its way to others. It doesn't stop with us. It bears fruit as it is shared. It grows as it is given away. This is the rhythm of abiding in God's love. As we abide, the home grows into a place of welcome, grace, hospitality, and beautiful harmony. It becomes a place where we can breathe! It becomes a blessing that we want to share with others.

Known by Fruit

Discipleship has a trajectory—to bear fruit (John 15:1). Faith has a purpose—to produce good fruit (15:4).

Following Jesus leads to a specific outcome, clarified here as "fruit that will last" (15:16).

The word "love" (agape) must be used to illuminate this holy fruit. We know what this love looks like. The love to which we are called is patient and kind. It is not arrogant or rude. It does not insist on its own way. It forgives and forgives again. It serves with more compassion and less judgment. It cultivates harmony, not monotony, unity rather than uniformity (See 1 Corinthians 13:4-8; Colossians 3:12-14). When Paul lists the fruit of the spirit in Galatians, the word "fruit" is singular. The first example of this fruit is love. This could be interpreted by saying that the fruit of the spirit is love, and the other virtues of joy, peace, patience, kindness, goodness, faithfulness, gentleness, and temperance are all descriptors of love (See Galatians 5:22-23).

Connecting to the idea of fruit that lasts, I think of how the apostle Paul concludes his poetic discourse on love by saying that "love never ends." Prophecies, knowledge, possessions, even faith, mean nothing without the fruit of love (1 Corinthians 13:1-8). How can we possibly love in this way? We can do so only as we abide, as we open our hearts to God's transforming love and allow this love to take up residence in our lives.

The fruit of love grows from branches that are connected to the vine. This metaphor imagines Christ as the vine and we are the branches. We can branch out into the world as long as we stay rooted in Christ. We all know the outcome of breaking off a branch from a vine. Fruit is no longer possible. If fruit is to come, the branch must stay connected to the source of nourishment. Again, abiding is key. In this passage, Jesus reveals this by example and witness.

To engage in some interpretive imagination, nature reveals branches in abundance with a multitude of sizes and shapes. From my backyard, I can see many trees and the way the branches fill the winter sky, with the light able to shine through. It is moving and inspiring. The multitude of interwoven connections is amazing to see and can teach us something more about love. Love speaks to the blessings of diversity and abundance. Love is the fruit that creates harmony over monotony and discord. Love connects us to something so much bigger than ourselves, even to something eternal.

If the goal were sameness and uniformity, there would be little need for the kind of love the scriptures proclaim—love that is patient, humble, forgiving, without arrogance and "insisting." This kind of love makes the diversity exhibited in nature and in the Body of Christ such a beautiful thing. I think of Jesus saying—and I paraphrase—"What good is it to love only those who are like you? Everyone can do that." As the church, we are called to a greater love than this (Matthew 5:46-48).

The Hard Part of Gardening and Discipleship

Pruning is a must. With this word, a great challenge is presented. If love is the expectation, pruning is required.

This act of pruning can sound harsh. The notion of branches being cut off and burned can be alarming and scary. However, we may miss the point if we assume this is a claim about the eternal life and death of souls. As we see consistently in John, judgment is not the goal; the gospel is an invitation for all to experience the blessings of eternal life, even now. It may be helpful to compare how the apostle Paul uses a similar metaphor. He points out that God can graft branches back in (Romans 11:17-24). God can give new life even out of the ashes. With a desire to fulfill this purpose, new life can be experienced and shared. Without this abiding, however, death remains.

The image of pruning can also be seen as a gift, making it possible for love to grow. Branches that crowd out fruit must be cut away if growth is to be cultivated. It is true in gardening and in our lives. If love is patient, we must work to remove impatience from our lives. If love is humble and does not insist on its own way, we must work on our temptations to be arrogant and judgmental.

To expand the metaphor, we must be willing to examine the proverbial log in our own eye before focusing too much on the speck in the eye of another (Luke 6:41-42). Pruning starts with us before we focus on others. As those who abide in Christ, we are called to be aware of the temptation to justify unholy temperaments by veiling them in a profane version of holiness. Arrogance and "insisting on our own way" are not the kinds of righteousness God wants from us. Division, schism, and judgment are not the witness that God wants the world to see from us. Be aware or Beware! (John 15:18). The warning is strong. If we are to fulfill God's calling upon our lives to bear good fruit, pruning is a must. And it starts with us.

To use another metaphor from Jesus, to focus on others is not only to build our home on sand but on the froth of the sea. John Wesley used this image when talking about basing our faith on our sense of orthodoxy, right opinion, or on a set of notions that we think is more rational or scriptural than what others have (See Wesley's Discourse 13, Sermon on the Mount). We are invited to participate in the making of a home and to do so on the solid rock of God's love.

A Love/Hate Relationship with the World

John likes to compare and contrast, using metaphors and symbolic references to communicate the gospel—light and dark, spirit and flesh, salvation and judgment—and in this chapter, love and hate. In this chapter, the word "hate" occurs eight times.

Interestingly, the word "love," translated from the Greek word "agape," is used nine times. In one other place, the Greek word "philia" is used, where we are told that the world would "love" us or "be fond of us" if we followed the ways "of the world" (John 15:19).

Jesus is not calling us to hate the world. Instead, this is a warning of how the world can hate us as we follow Jesus. The word translated as "world" (cosmos) is used to define the order of all creation. The opposite of this word would be chaos, disorder, and being uncreative. In the stories of creation, we hear that the "cosmos" in its original state was good, even very good. But something happened in our understanding of faith-cosmology. Creation/the world/the larger system for how things hold together became corrupted and disconnected. We might think of branches being torn from the vine. To be cosmopolitan is defined by moving forward rather than upward, more interested in personal pleasure and gain than in bearing good fruit. To be worldly is marked by advancing personal desires without concern for virtue and "fruit that last." This is what happens when the branch is severed from the vine.

Especially to those put into positions of power and privilege, the temptation can be strong to give in, to gaslight, to protect, to divide, and all in the name of a temporary (less-than-cosmic) order seen as chaos from a higher and holy perspective. If one wants the world to be "fond" of them, then give into this temptation.

And please note, those in the church are not immune. Leaders in the church may be most susceptible to abuse and the temptation to use spiritual forms of cosmetics to make abuse appear as righteousness. Some may seem self-aware but cannot connect this awareness to the larger calling on our lives and are thus blind to the warning. In this light, we are the ones told by our Savior to be aware or beware. This warning is for us!

The world hates us when we are most fully aware. And we need to know what the word "hate" means. The word used here (miseo) does not carry the sense of being an adversary we sometimes associate with hatred. Rather, it compares one thing to another regarding moral and spiritual value. To hate is to "love less," as defined in *Strong's Concordance*. To hate is to subordinate in terms of rank. It can be used positively and negatively. It can mean to be "put down" or as a call to "rank something lower." Jesus, for example, says that we cannot be his disciples until we hate our family and even our own life (See Luke 14:26). Of course, we are to love our family and honor them, but we are not to give allegiance to them over God.

All of this talk of hate and the world must be held in tension with the places in John where we are told that Christ is Savior of the world (John 4:42) and the light of the world (John 8:12). We are told that God loves the world and did not come to condemn or judge the world (John 3:16-17, 12:47). We are not called to "hate" in the sense of causing harm or despising others. That is never to be our witness. At the same time, once again, we must be aware that the systems of the world can react to us in this way. There are times when the word carries this punch. It can even come from inside the church as we get caught up in the world's temptations. So, be careful out there even as you boldly go into the world with the love of Christ!

A Spirit Connection

The chapter concludes with a word about the Holy Spirit. In short, Jesus wants us to know we will not be left without help. The Counselor or Advocate (paraclete) will come (John 15:26). This word is unique to John's Gospel. It means to "call alongside" (para = alongside; klete = to call). The Spirit will walk alongside us and gently call, comfort, and advocate for us. With the image of being at our side, we can sense that this relationship is never forced or coerced. We are not pulled from ahead or pushed from behind. The Holy Spirit stands with us, alongside us. The Holy Spirit abides. We can again think of the image of a friend, of one with us rather than over us.

And then, in this same verse, another name is given, the Spirit of truth (pneuma tes aletheia). This name is used in two other places as well (John 14:17, 16:13). Truth, in this context, means to "uncover" or "reveal" what is good and life-giving. Christ, as the Word made flesh, is truth, and the Spirit gives witness (John 1:14, 17:17, 15:26). To walk in truth is to "love one another." To "rejoice in truth" is to practice love that is patient, kind, and humble (1 Corinthians 13:4-8, Ephesians 4:1-3, Colossians 3:12-17). The Spirit of truth reveals while the ways of the world try to conceal and hide, often by putting down, hating, and judging by criteria that keep us from considering another's calling, character, and commitment to Christ. Truth is revealed when we abide in love.

To come full circle, the Word became flesh and dwelt among us, full of grace and truth (John 1:14). Truth is revealed as God plops down in our midst and makes a home in us and with us. We are invited into a home full of all that reveals the love of God.

Joy Abiding

Jesus said these things so that we would know joy (John 15:11). We might say he wants us to be "happy," although that word is a bit casual for what is offered here. "Happiness," as we often use it, is circumstantial. In other words, happiness depends on the circumstances of our lives. When things are going well, we are happy. When things are not going well, it is hard to be happy. In this sense, God does not expect us to always be happy. We can, however, know joy in all circumstances. Joy is a gift of the Spirit. Joy is a deep sense of contentment and well-being, present and available in all circumstances. Happiness comes and goes; joy abides! Joy abides within and fills us with the truth that God is with us, and nothing can separate us from God's love (Romans 8:38-39). May you know this joy! May it rock your theological world!

Reflection Questions:

What transformations of understanding are sparked by the story of a pastor being more approachable? How do the concepts of dwelling and abiding speak to our understanding of God? What do they say about how we are to treat one another?

How do the rhythms of love work in your life? How might these blessings be cultivated in your life? What is the love to which we are called? How might we pervert this understanding?

What is the fruit that we are called to bear? What relationship between the vine and branches is needed? How do we avoid fruit that is harmful and even deadly? How does this metaphor speak to the blessings of diversity within creation and within the body of Christ?

What temperaments or dispositions need to be pruned? What virtues need to be cultivated if we are to be faithful and fruitful? What resources, or means of grace, are available to us through the church? How can we heed the warning given here?

The home made by God is described as being "full of grace and truth" (John 1:14). In debates within the church, sometimes a critique is given against those who want grace without truth or truth without grace. It may be misleading to see these in polarity. Seeing these dimensions of faith as enhancing each other may be more fruitful. Truth illuminates or reveals the blessings of grace and vice versa. Truth is revealed in actions that are life-giving and bear good fruit. If such actions are not full of grace, then they conceal and hide rather than reveal and illuminate.

At one point in the Gospel of John, Jesus calls the evil one "the father of lies." Evil and deception go together. Lies destroy and divide. Truth unites and brings life to relationships. In this sense, truth is revealed as we find ways to love even those with whom we disagree. With this understanding, truth can be concealed with judgment and the creation of hard lines in the sand. Living fully in grace and trust is hard work in this world. We could say it is impossible without the Holy Spirit, the Spirit of truth. What is truth? What is the relationship between grace and truth? What is the role of the Holy Spirit in the way we give witness to God's grace and truth?

Lesson 6

Savior, Like A Shepherd, Lead Us
Lesson by LaToya Juanita Shepherd and Mike McSpadden

About the Lesson Writers:

LaToya Shepherd is a local pastor serving Mission United Methodist Church in Fort Smith, Arkansas. LaToya is the mother of four: Christa Marie (Jaivin), Rachel Jenay (Kiera), Leonard Jonathan, and fur baby TJ. She is a grandmother of three: Jenesis Marie, Edyn Juanita Jenay, and Leonard Ezquiel Ramon'. LaToya loves to sing, write, serve the church/community, bargain shop, and feed her friends and family.

Mike McSpadden is a retired school administrator in Alma, Arkansas. He frequently writes leadership material for educators, pastors, and business people.

Scripture Lesson:
Psalm 23:1-6 (Amplified Version)

The Amplified Translation of the scripture provides expanded or amplified meanings of words in parentheses.

> *The Lord is my Shepherd [to feed, to guide and to shield me],*
> *I shall not want.*
>
> *He lets me lie down in green pastures;*
> *He leads me beside the still and quiet waters.*

He refreshes and restores my soul (life);
He leads me in the paths of righteousness for
His name's sake.

Even though I walk through the [sunless] valley of the
shadow of death,
I fear no evil, for You are with me;
Your rod [to protect] and Your staff [to guide], they
comfort and console me.

You prepare a table before me in the presence of my
enemies.
You have anointed and refreshed my head with oil;
My cup overflows.

Surely goodness and mercy and unfailing love shall
follow me all the days of my life,
And I shall dwell forever [throughout all my days] in the
house and in the presence of the Lord.

Introduction

The scriptures often speak of the people of God and the followers of Jesus Christ as sheep. Isaiah 40:11 declares, "The Lord God will feed his flock like a Shepherd." Hebrews 13:20 references Jesus as the great Shepherd of the sheep. In John 10, Jesus describes himself as the Good Shepherd and talks about his relationship to the sheep. He says, "I am the Good Shepherd, and I know [without any doubt those who are] My own and my own know Me [and have a deep, personal relationship with Me].

Psalm 23 is a scripture passage often recited and memorized for multiple occasions in the church's life. In this simple lesson and psalm, we can use David's experience and descriptions of the Lord as his Shepherd to inspire, encourage, and even guide.

Psalm 23 was the first scripture I memorized as a child at the direction of my paternal grandmother, Juanita Grace. Psalm 23 is the scripture I still remember when my memory fails, when life is stressful, and I need to recall who is the Lord of my soul. I have always found it intriguing, especially as a pastor (shepherd), that the one who was the little-shepherd-boy-turned-king found it beneficial and necessary to pen words that declare the ultimate Shepherd for him is the Lord. I use this psalm of David as a practical reminder for myself and others to whom we believe in and entrust our lives. The Lord IS my Shepherd.

As sheep (followers of Jesus Christ), the encouragement from this scripture is that because of our relationship with the Shepherd, we have access to the presence of the Shepherd, **provision** from the Shepherd, and **protection** of the Shepherd.

As shepherds (leaders and pastors in the church and marketplace), one can use the natural example of how a shepherd acts towards and cares for those in their flock as an example of how the sheep can benefit from the **presence, provision,** and **protection** of their leaders.

Reflections for the Sheep
By LaToya Juanita Shepherd

Presence

The Lord is my Shepherd [to feed, to guide and to shield me].

The psalmist declares in the first verse what role the Lord plays in his life. David says the Lord is his Shepherd. This immediately gives the reader a sense of David's confidence in whom he is speaking about, which defines the relationship. One could also ascertain from the words of this verse that David feels the presence of the Shepherd in his life. A shepherd is responsible for being present and available to tend to the flock. The Lord, as the Shepherd of our lives and souls, is active and present in every aspect. Just as David declares, the believer should name the Lord as the Shepherd of our lives and souls.

The presence of the Lord is not always noted by a specific emotion or feeling. The presence of the Lord is substantiated by knowing the scripture and relying upon what Jesus promised his disciples after he gave them their commission. Jesus promised that he would be with his disciples always until the end of the world. If we are truly Jesus' disciples, this promise is ours as well. In the words of the saints I grew up around, "You just know that you know that you know. That's faith."

The Lord's presence has been a source of stability

and security for me, as it is for many others. There have been times when I have been away from family and close friends. There have been times when I had people I could rely on, yet the guiding and feeding of the Lord, my Shepherd, was more than any human presence could contribute. Like David, we believers can declare, "The Lord IS my Shepherd!"

As followers of Jesus Christ, we have the promised presence of the Holy Spirit (Matthew 28:20) and Jesus Christ as our heavenly advocate (John 14:15-17).

Provision

> *He lets me lie down in green pastures;*
> *He leads me beside the still and quiet waters.*
>
> *He refreshes and restores my soul (life);*
> *He leads me in the paths of righteousness*
> *for His name's sake.*
>
> *You prepare a table before me in the presence of my enemies.*
> *You have anointed and refreshed my head with oil;*
> *My cup overflows.*

In the natural relationship between a shepherd and sheep, the shepherd is responsible for providing for the sheep. David declares that the Lord, his Shepherd, indeed provides. What the Shepherd provides is a restful, peaceful, and quiet experience for David. Whether one looks at this as David lying down and being refreshed in the green pastures and next to still waters or as an emotional or psychological state of being, David is being refreshed and experiencing refreshment of his body and soul.

David also makes an important point in saying that the leadership the Shepherd provides is not just for David's benefit but for the sake of the Shepherd's name. Some provisions are also carried out in the plain sight of those who may be enemies—or haters, in the modern vernacular. The Shepherd does not provide meager provisions. The provisions are overflowing and well-prepared, and they continue to speak to the character of the Shepherd and the Shepherd's love and care.

There are times in our lives when we need rest and replenishment. There are also times when those around us can benefit from seeing the abundance of oil being poured into our lives by our Savior. I have experienced peace and quiet in the middle of chaos, not because I had it within me but because I was able to remember that the Shepherd of my soul offered exactly what David described in this psalm. Even being amid folk who are not on our side will not prevent our Lord from blessing and taking care of us. The Lord IS my Shepherd!

As followers of Jesus Christ, we have access to provision, rest, and peace that can be found in our relationship with Jesus Christ (Matthew 11:28-29) and our dependence upon the Holy Spirit (John 14:27).

Protection

Even though I walk through the [sunless] valley of the shadow of death,
I fear no evil, for You are with me;

Your rod [to protect] and Your staff [to guide], they comfort and console me.

Surely goodness and mercy and unfailing love shall follow me all the days of my life,
And I shall dwell forever [throughout all my days] in the house and in the presence of the Lord.

One of the most important aspects of a shepherd's job is to keep the sheep safe. David says of his Shepherd that, even when faced with darkness and the shadow of death, he is not fearful. He has the presence, provision, and protection of the Shepherd. The shepherd has the tangible tools to protect the sheep and, ultimately, the authority and power for the necessary protection. This protection and provision are not temporary; it is lifelong! David declares that goodness and mercy are his lifelong companions and that he chooses to be in the house and presence of the Lord for the rest of his life.

Life can sometimes take us into some scary places. The death of loved ones, sickness, war, financial troubles, emotional issues, spiritual battles, injustice, family problems, relationship issues, political unrest, and yes, religious disputes, and many other scenarios can cause us to feel like we are in the valley of the shadow of death. Yet, the Shepherd is with us. Our faith does not keep us from entering the valley of the shadow of death. Our faith and the protection of the Shepherd keep us from buckling to fear and evil.

There have been some moments in my life when I have thought the condition I was in, mentally, physically, and emotionally, would surely lead to my death, literally or spiritually. But the words of David in Psalm 23 welled up in my soul and reminded me that the rod and staff of the Shepherd were present to protect, guide, console, and comfort me. The Lord IS my Shepherd!

As followers of Jesus Christ, we have the assurance that after this life is over, we will live with Christ forever. However, we can have a life of abundance while we live on earth (John 10:10).

Reflections for a Shepherd
By Mike McSpadden

The concept of leaders as shepherds is not as prevalent in our society today as it once was. The Bible, for example, is full of verses about shepherds and sheep. But when we travel around today, we don't see many shepherds in pastures tending their sheep. However, this concept is a fundamental and critical aspect of leadership, so I want to address it here.

Presence

You can't shepherd from your office. You can't shepherd by email. You can't shepherd by memos. You can't shepherd by texts. A shepherd has to be with the sheep! Leadership is fundamentally giving the people you lead what they need, so how do you know what they need if you are not with them? Some sheep might need care, some might need correction, and some might need extra food, and the only way to know this is by being with them. Shepherds smell like sheep.

Provision

Shepherds know which pastures to lead the flock to, where they can find water, how long to stay in a pasture, etc. John Maxwell says:

> A leader KNOWS the way, GOES the way, and SHOWS the way.[12]

Leaders have a vision, and they have a plan to execute that vision. Leaders don't allow the organization to simply exist; they are constantly looking for ways to improve, make things better, and take care of the needs of their people.

Protection

In the Bible, David recounts how he killed a lion and a bear while tending the sheep. In the old days, shepherds were constantly on the alert for predators since sheep are basically defenseless. At night, shepherds would find a shelter of some sort, and then

---

[12] John C. Maxwell, *150 Essential Insights on Leadership* (Harvest House Publishers, 2021).

they would lay down at the entrance. Basically, they were saying, *If you want to harm my sheep, you are going to have to go through me first!* We live in a culture that attacks, criticizes, and second-guesses every aspect of practically every organization. Every church, school, business, athletic team, non-profit, and governmental entity is constantly eviscerated by anyone with a keyboard or microphone. (No matter who wins the Super Bowl Sunday night, the losing coach will be blamed for the loss.) In this environment, leaders absolutely MUST protect the people in their organization from attack. As human beings, we need to feel safe. When people are in an insecure environment, their morale suffers, their productivity suffers, their attendance suffers, and eventually, they leave.

As a leader, if you aren't present and don't provide and protect, you really aren't a shepherd; you are a hired hand. Honestly, you won't be a shepherd for very long because the sheep will be destroyed, starve to death, be stolen, or leave. A leader with no followers is not a leader; a shepherd with no sheep is not a shepherd.

We all need to evaluate our own leadership constantly, and we can do that by examining the people we lead. How are they mentally, physically, emotionally, and spiritually? Do they feel threatened and insecure? Are they growing, thriving, and improving? Are new people being added or are people leaving?

Keep being present. Keep providing. Keep protecting. Keep leading.

> *The good shepherd lays down his life for the sheep. The hired hand is not the shepherd and does not own the sheep. So when he sees the wolf coming, he abandons the sheep and runs away. Then the wolf attacks the flock and scatters it. The man runs away because he is a hired hand and cares nothing for the sheep.*
>
> **John 10: 11-13 (NIV)**

Reflection Questions:

How have you experienced the presence of the Holy Spirit working in your life?

How do you engage in activities that provide your natural body with rest and refreshment?

What are the spiritual disciplines (prayer, fasting, worship, etc.) you employ regularly to encourage spiritual refreshment and encouragement?

Have there been times when you believe the Holy Spirit protected you from a certain situation or outcome?

How do you let those you are trusted to lead know that you have their best interest at heart?

Does your leadership reflect the character and integrity of a servant leader or a Shepherd?

Hymn for Reference

Savior, Like a Shepherd Lead Us

Music by William Bradbury, 1859, Words by Dorothy Bradbury

Savior, like a shepherd lead us, much we need Thy tender care;
In Thy pleasant pastures feed us, for our use Thy folds prepare.
Blessed Jesus, blessed Jesus! Thou hast bought us, Thine we are.
Blessed Jesus, blessed Jesus! Thou hast bought us, Thine we are.

We are Thine, Thou dost befriend us, be the Guardian of our way;
Keep Thy flock, from sin defend us, seek us when we go astray.
Blessed Jesus, blessed Jesus! Hear, O hear us when we pray.
Blessed Jesus, blessed Jesus! Hear, O hear us when we pray.

Thou hast promised to receive us, poor and sinful though we be;
Thou hast mercy to relieve us, grace to cleanse and pow'r to free.
Blessed Jesus, blessed Jesus! We will early turn to Thee.
Blessed Jesus, blessed Jesus! We will early turn to Thee.

Early let us seek Thy favor, early let us do Thy will;
Blessed Lord and only Savior, with Thy love our bosoms fill.
Blessed Jesus, blessed Jesus! Thou hast loved us, love us still.
Blessed Jesus, blessed Jesus! Thou hast loved us, love us still.

Lesson 7

The God of Hagar
Lesson by Melanie Tubbs

About the Lesson Writer:

Rev. Melanie Tubbs is an ordained elder in the Arkansas Conference of the United Methodist Church serving as senior pastor of Jacksonville First United Methodist Church. Melanie is a graduate of ILIFF School of Theology and taught history in high school and college before entering full-time ministry.

Scripture Lesson:
Genesis 21:8-21

> *The boy grew and stopped nursing. On the day he stopped nursing, Abraham prepared a huge banquet. Sarah saw Hagar's son laughing, the one Hagar the Egyptian had borne to Abraham. So, she said to Abraham, "Send this servant away with her son! This servant's son won't share the inheritance with my son Isaac." This upset Abraham terribly because the boy is his son. God said to Abraham, "Don't be upset about the boy and your servant. Do everything Sarah tells you to do because your descendants will be traced through Isaac. But I will make of your servant's son a great nation too, because he is also your descendant." Abraham got up early in the morning, took some bread and a flask of water, and gave it to Hagar. He put the boy in her shoulder sling and sent her away. She left and wandered through the desert near Beer-sheba. Finally, the water in the flask ran out, and*

she put the boy down under one of the desert shrubs. She walked away from him about as far as a bow shot and sat down, telling herself, I can't bear to see the boy die. She sat at a distance, cried out in grief, and wept. God heard the boy's cries, and God's messenger called to Hagar from heaven and said to her, "Hagar! What's wrong? Don't be afraid. God had heard the boy's cries over there. Get up, pick up the boy, and take him by the hand because I will make of him a great nation." Then God opened her eyes, and she saw a well. She went over, filled the water flask, and gave the boy a drink. God remained with the boy; he grew up, lived in the desert, and became an expert archer. He lived in the Paran desert, and his mother found him an Egyptian wife.

Genesis 21:8-21 (CEB)

Starting in Chapter 12 of the book of Genesis, Abraham becomes the central character in the story of God's relationship with God's people. God first tells Abraham to leave everything he has ever known, taking all that he has and everyone in his household, and go to an unknown place where God is sending him. He does. During a famine at this new location, Abraham goes to Egypt to survive, where he becomes fabulously wealthy by passing his wife off as his sister and allowing her to be taken into the Pharaoh's haram. When God sends plagues on Pharoah and his household for taking a married woman, Abraham is kicked out of Egypt and goes back to the land of Canaan, taking his newly gotten wealth with him. God reaffirms his promise to Abraham that he would have land, descendants, and blessings, but this seems unlikely because Abraham and his wife, Sarah, are far too old to have children.

After years of still not conceiving a child, in desperation for an heir, Sarah offers her Egyptian slave, Hagar, to Abraham as a concubine. Hagar, a woman without rights or control of even her own body, was given to this much older man by another woman and had no choice but to allow her body to be used as an incubator so Sarah could have a child that she would legally be able to claim and control. But even though it is Sarah's decision to send Hagar to Abraham, when Hagar does become pregnant, Sarah abuses Hagar so badly that this woman without choices feels her only option is to run away into a dangerous and unforgiving desert. God comes to Hagar in the wilderness and tells her to return to the clan so she will have resources and protection in the only way available to her, so she does as she is told. Hagar has a son and names him Ishmael. This elevates Hagar from a slave or even a concubine. She is now the wife who provided Abraham, a very wealthy man, with a male heir, which is much harder for Sarah to live with than she had imagined.

Hagar has always fascinated me. She is said to be an Egyptian woman, so we assume she came with Abraham and Sarah when they left Egypt. She may have been a gift to Sarah from Pharoah as a way to make amends for adding her to his haram when he thought she was unmarried. That means Hagar knew about the ruse Abraham and Sarah had pulled with the Pharoah passing Sarah off as Abraham's sister. Hagar knew Sarah had spent time in the Pharoah's haram. That had to be uncomfortable for Sarah.

When Hagar becomes pregnant, Sarah complains that Hagar looks down on her and doesn't treat her with the respect Sarah believes she deserves. I always wonder if that is just because Hagar is able to conceive and Sarah isn't or if maybe there is a little bit of the "I know what you did" thing going on. Not only did Hagar know what Abraham and Sarah had done, but now Hagar is pregnant with Abraham's baby, something Sarah had never been able to do. Maybe that's one of the reasons Sarah is so hard on Hagar; even though Sarah is the powerful first wife of a wealthy and powerful man, she knows that Hagar knows the dirty secrets of her past.

Scripture states simply that Sarah is abusive to Hagar after Hagar becomes pregnant, and so Hagar runs away. While Hagar is on the run, God speaks to her. And not just a little command; God has a pretty long conversation as far as conversations with God go. Not only does God tell Hagar that she is to go back and put up with Sarah, but God also tells her that she will have a son whom she should call Ishmael and who will be the foundation of his own nation.

Scripture says Hagar answered God, called God by name, and declared God to be El Roi, the "God who sees me." It is a pretty significant declaration, knowing that she is Egyptian and Egyptians have their own gods—and lots of them. Yet, there in the desert, pregnant and on the run, Hagar named the God of Abraham the "God who sees me." God reaffirms the covenant with Abraham that God will give him land, descendants, and blessings, and at this point in the story, after Ishmael has already been born, God tells Abraham that it will actually be Sarah who will bear the son of promise. God also informs Abraham not to worry because God will bless Ishmael as well. Later, God again appears to Abraham in the form of three messengers and tells him that Sarah, now ninety, is about to get pregnant. Sarah and Abraham laugh hard at this, but one year later, Sarah gives birth to a son and names him Isaac, which means laughter.

This development of a new heir born to Sarah and Abraham presents a problem for Hagar and Ishmael. Where did that leave Ishmael in Abraham's line? Sarah, a woman who spent ninety years unable to have a child and became so desperate for one that she sent another woman to her husband's bed to conceive, immediately becomes defensive, wanting to be certain that nothing interferes with the inheritance of her own son. Ishmael had once been the answer to Abraham and Sarah's prayers. Now Hagar and Ishmael are, at the very least, an intrusion and possibly even a threat.

Three years later, there is a big party celebrating the fact that Isaac has survived infancy and is old enough to be weaned. At the party, Sarah sees Ishmael, now in his teens, laughing. We often interpret this to mean that Ishmael was laughing at Isaac, but that part was probably edited into the scripture much later after the original story was written. It may just have been that Sarah saw Ishmael laughing and having a good time at the party, which annoyed her. But whatever the reason, Sarah sees Ishmael laughing and tells Abraham that both Hagar and Ishmael must go.

One has to wonder if Sarah has been looking for a reason to throw Hagar and Ishmael out ever since Isaac was born. The opportunity presents itself at the celebration of Isaac's weaning, and Sarah doesn't waste any time running to tell Abraham that Hagar, the slave woman, and her son have to go. After all, Isaac had survived infancy, so they didn't need the backup plan—which was Ishmael—anymore. He would just be a threat to Isaac's inheritance, and nothing is more important to Sarah than her son being the sole heir to Abraham.

Abraham didn't want to send Hagar and Ishmael away; scripture says it was very distressing to him. But God speaks to Abraham that night and tells him to do what Sarah says. "Send them out and I will make a nation of Ishmael too because he is your son." Abraham gives Hagar a loaf of bread and a bottle of water the next morning and sends her and Ishmael away. Not a great send-off for your first-born son. Hagar and Ishmael were said to be wandering about in the wilderness, a rough and unforgiving landscape.

It's important to note that by forcing her slave to go

to Abraham's bed, Sarah herself was responsible for elevating Hagar to the station of wife. But here, when Sarah is feeling more confident and powerful after the birth of her own son, she refers to Hagar as a slave again. Sarah is very purposefully using her words to try to remove any claims that Hagar or her son might have in Abraham's family.

One has to wonder why this story is even included in the stories of Abraham. If Isaac is the promised son anyway, why tell this side story about a son who would just be cast out? Except for the fact that, years later, when Abraham dies, Ishmael is said to be present with Isaac, and the two sons bury their father together. Then we get a short genealogy report of Ishmael's descendants at that time, but we don't hear any more of his story in the Bible. So why include it at all? Telling the story of Abraham throwing his first son out into the desert certainly doesn't make Abraham and Sarah look good. And to abandon family members, people under your care and responsibility, was actually considered not just immoral but also illegal in their culture. So why is it included in scripture?

Once again alone and desperate, this time not just her but with her son, Hagar believes that she is about to witness the slow, painful death of Ishmael from exposure and lack of water. But just like when she ran into the desert while pregnant, God shows up to speak directly to her: "Hagar! What's wrong? Don't be afraid."

God comforts Hagar, assures her that her son would be a great nation, and points her to a well, saving the lives of her and her son.

Even though Ishmael isn't the child who would carry forward God's covenant promises, God has a plan for Hagar and Ishmael. And we know this is true because we get that genealogy list after Abraham dies in Genesis 25. We also know that he must have stayed in touch with his half-brother Isaac since, in a world without Facebook or text messages, Ishmael is present to bury his father. And I'm guessing that Ishmael took very good care of his mother, Hagar, who had gone through so much. He lived 137 years and had twelve sons.

In fact, maybe Hagar is the point of the story and not Ishmael. After all, even though the messengers talking to Abraham did respond to the fact that Sarah laughed, God never sought out Sarah to have a chat with her. But God speaks directly to Hagar, not once, but twice. If face time with God is a mark of importance in the Bible, Hagar is one of the more important characters. So why Hagar?

The main theme of all the stories in Genesis is the fulfillment of the promise God made to Abraham. But by including Hagar's story, we are reminded that God still remembers the rest of God's people. Throughout the story of God's chosen people, those in the direct line from Abraham through David and to Christ are also included in the stories of lesser players. The minor players. The sidenotes. No matter where their stories go, God is always with them. Jacob declares he sees the face of God in his brother, Esau, who had his birthright in the lineage stolen and was replaced by younger Jacob. Maybe there is more to the Bible than just the direct institutional chosen path; maybe sometimes the exiles and the sidenotes are the point.

God is the God of second sons, outcast relatives, the lost, and the enslaved. God is not just the God of the big names of the Bible, the heroes of our faith, but also of the side characters and the forgotten ones. There are so many who can find their own story in the story of Hagar. The exploited worker, the other woman, the second wife, the sex abuse survivor, the surrogate mom, the resident alien, the single mother, the homeless woman, the woman with no identity but the one she had in association with men. Do we, the church community, remember the Hagars in our stories? Do we see them in our neighborhoods? What about when you are the Hagar and not the Sarah? Or maybe even more importantly, what about when you are the Sarah, and the story is about how you treat the Hagars?

Hagar and Ishmael are cast out. And while God doesn't prevent that from happening, in the middle of the fear and brokenness of where they are, God meets them in the wilderness where they were cast and provides care in the present and hope and prosperity in the future.

Humans bring distress and alienation, but God is ever-present, even in the margins. God is a way-maker and a provider for all those whom society casts out. God is at work among the forgotten and the outcasts. God holds up the refugees and makes a new way. God may be leading the chosen and promised through the main story of the Bible, but God also sits with the lost and the thrown away in their wilderness.

No matter where you are, who is against you, or what your circumstances may be, God is still El Roi, "the God who sees me."

Reflection Questions:

Have you ever been jealous of someone's joy? Sarah is angry because Ishmael is enjoying himself at HER son's party—how dare he? He should know his place. How does our jealousy impact our relationships and our ability or inability to be in relationship with God?

What do you think of when you hear the word "haughty"? Think of a time or situation where someone behaved unvirtuously because they believed themselves to be higher in station or class. In Sarah's case, she felt less than because she couldn't conceive, and once she does conceive, this new station comes with new power that she uses to cause harm. How do we react when we are privileged with power over someone else?

Who are some other people God has conversations with in the Bible? How do the conversation and the results of the conversation with Hagar compare to the other times God speaks to humans? Specifically, how do Hagar's conversations with God compare to the conversations God has with Abraham? With the woman at the well (John 4)?

Ishmael and Isaac both bury their father. We know nothing of the in-between time from being cast out to the burial. Much of our Christian faith is rooted in forgiveness and reconciliation. Is there someone in your life you've made peace with or a situation you look back on with regret because forgiveness didn't happen? How can remembering you are a worthy, redeemed, and loved child of God help you in your own relationships? What can the story of Abraham, Sarah, Isaac, Hagar, and Ishmael teach us about our relationships?

Has there been a time when you were exiled or cast out, possibly feeling profound despair or hopelessness, and God spoke to you in the wilderness? When have you felt alone, abandoned, or not seen, but God pointed you to a well?

Lesson 8

Voice to the Voiceless
Lesson by Bill Sardin

About the Lesson Writer:

Bill Sardin serves as the pastor of the First United Methodist Church of Morrilton, Arkansas. On his YouTube channel "Long Hair, Tattoos and No Shoes, " he shares an online daily devotion, Monday-Friday." Bill has been married to his wife, Kimberly, for 25 years. They have two sons, Wryen and Wesley, and their border collie, Oreo. Oreo runs the Sardin household.

Scripture:
John 20:11-18

> *But Mary stood weeping outside the tomb. As she wept, she bent over to look into the tomb; and she saw two angels in white, sitting where the body of Jesus had been lying, one at the head and the other at the feet. They said to her, "Woman, why are you weeping?" She said to them, "They have taken away my Lord, and I do not know where they have laid him." When she had said this, she turned around and saw Jesus standing there, but she did not know that it was Jesus. Jesus said to her, "Woman, why are you weeping? Whom are you looking for?" Supposing him to be the gardener, she said to him, "Sir, if you have carried him away, tell me where you have laid him, and I will take him away." Jesus said to her, "Mary!" She turned and said to him in Hebrew, "Rabbouni!" (which means Teacher). Jesus said to her,*

> "Do not hold on to me, because I have not yet ascended to the Father. But go to my brothers and say to them, 'I am ascending to my Father and your Father, to my God and your God.'" Mary Magdalene went and announced to the disciples, "I have seen the Lord"; and she told them that he had said these things to her.
>
> John 20:11-18 (NRSV)

The Enduring Fascination with Mary Magdalene

She is perhaps one of the most recognizable women in scripture, yet she only appears in a few verses. This is Mary Magdalene, a woman who has attracted curiosity, speculation, conspiracy theories, and scandal. Mary Magdalene has inspired books, television specials, and even a retraction from the Vatican. Yet truthfully, we know very little about this woman who has fascinated Christians for nearly 2,000 years.

If you mention the name of Mary Magdalene, even to a person who has never read the Bible, there will be a spark of recognition. Millions of readers learned the name Mary Magdalene from Dan Brown's book "The DaVinci Code." Others may know Mary from the Biblical "documentaries" that can be found on cable networks. Speculating that Jesus had a special relationship with Mary fueled our cultural fascination.

The fascination with Mary Magdalene is not a modern phenomenon. There are extra-biblical writings about Mary that date back to the first century. Three ancient documents testify to early curiosity about Mary.

There are the Gnostic gospels of *The Gospel of Mary* and *The Gospel of Philip*.

There are no complete copies of "The Gospel of Mary." From the fragments, it is clear that the gospel sets Mary up as the primary disciple. As with most Gnostic writing, *The Gospel of Mary* primarily focuses on escaping the material to enter into the spiritual that is accomplished through special spiritual knowledge.

The Gospel of Philip is also a Gnostic text. This extra-biblical gospel gained worldwide notice because of a fragment that mentions Mary Magdalene. The fragment was translated as "Jesus often kissed Mary on the mouth." The fragment generated speculation that Mary and Jesus were married. However, a Gnostic practice was to place a kiss on another's mouth to breathe spiritual knowledge into another. This practice usually only occurs between men. Most scholars agree that the kisses between Jesus and Mary in Philip's gospel were not sexual but intended to establish Mary as an apostle along with the 12.

Both Gnostic gospels were written nearly 200 years after Christ. They were both rejected for inclusion in the canon of the New Testament and deemed heretical. What makes them of interest for our purposes is that each shows that the tradition of Mary having a special place in Jesus' ministry and the birth of Christianity goes back to the church's very beginnings. This isn't a modern phenomenon but a genuine part of Christian DNA.

The Real Scandal with Mary Magdalene

To have a woman of this importance would have been unique during this period. It would have been almost unheard of in Near Eastern cultures like Palestine. It would not take long for the status of Mary Magdalene to garner a reaction from the church.

For centuries, Mary of Magdala has been identified as a prostitute. That identification most likely began with a homily preached by Pope Gregory the Great on September 14, 591. In the homily, Pope Gregory pronounced that the prostitute that washed Christ's feet with her hair in Luke 7, Mary of Bethany, Lazarus' sister, and Mary of Magdala were the same.

Since 591, Mary is characterized as a repentant prostitute. Mary is portrayed as a prostitute in art, books, and movies, even to the present. There is no evidence of malicious intent on the part of Pope Gregory in his characterization of Mary. While Gregory's portrayal of Mary makes for a beautiful story of redemption, Mary does not deserve to carry another person's sins throughout history.

What led to Pope Gregory's conclusion on Mary of Magdala's identity? More than likely, it was the proximity of Luke's telling of the sinful woman washing Jesus's feet in Luke 7:37-50 and the first appearance of Mary Magdalene in Luke 8:2. Another possible influence on Pope Gregory could have been John 12:1-8. In this passage, Mary of Bethany, the sister of Lazarus and Martha, anoints Jesus' feet with expensive perfume and then dries his feet with her hair.

It is not hard to imagine how Pope Gregory could conclude that these three women were the same person. Mary's introduction in Luke immediately follows the story of the sinful woman. Luke's account of the anointing of Jesus' feet and John's are startlingly similar. For Gregory, it must have seemed like a logical leap that they were all the same person.

Let's pause momentarily, examine the two Luke passages, and then move to the John passage. In Luke 7:37, the woman is identified only as a sinner. She is never given a name. She is simply referred to as "a woman." Pope Gregory links her to Mary because Mary of Magdala is introduced immediately following this story and because of how Mary was introduced.

In Luke 8:2, Mary is introduced this way:

> ...*Mary, called Magdalene, from whom seven demons had gone out.*

Pope Gregory determined that the seven demons that had gone out of Mary Magdalene symbolized the seven deadly sins:

> *She whom Luke calls the sinful woman, whom John calls Mary, we believe to be the Mary from whom seven devils were ejected according to Mark.*
>
> **(Pope Gregory, 23rd Homily)**

Most theologians today disagree with Gregory. It is more likely that Mary of Magdala was dealing with some mental illness than the symbolism that Gregory asserts. The idea that the woman in Luke 7 and Mary are the same person is just speculation with no evidence in the text.

The stories of the woman in Luke 7 and Mary of Bethany anointing Jesus' feet in John 10 show striking similarities on the surface. Both stories have a woman anointing Jesus' feet with expensive perfume. They both include drying Jesus' feet with the woman's hair. However, this is where the similarities end.

In Luke's Gospel, the woman washes Jesus' feet as an act of repentance. She knows that she is a sinner and has come looking for redemption. Additionally, the woman was drying her tears from Jesus' feet with her hair.

Mary of Bethany, in John's Gospel, was almost certainly washing Jesus' feet in an act of gratitude. In John 12:1, we are reminded that Jesus had raised Mary's brother Lazarus from the dead. Then, in just two verses, in John 12:3, Mary begins to wash Jesus' feet. Finally, Mary of Bethany dries the perfume from Jesus' feet with her hair.

Despite the similarities in the two stories, a close reading reveals that Mary of Bethany and the woman in Luke 7 are not the same person. John 12 and Luke 7 also tell the story of two different events. Luke and John use similar events to teach their readers something about Jesus, but the events and the woman differ.

This leaves the question, are Mary Magdalene and Mary of Bethany the same woman? The answer to this question is a definitive "NO." Magdalene is not a surname. Instead, Magdalene is a distortion of the identifier "of Magdala." Both women were distinguished by their place of birth. The Mary we find in John 12 lived in Bethany, approximately 2 miles from Jerusalem. Mary Magdalene was from the village of Magdala, which is nearly 70 miles north of Jerusalem. These two women were not even from the same region, much less the same person. The two women shared the same first name, which is unsurprising since Mary was one of the most common female names in Israel.

The First Mention of Mary of Magdala

Mary of Magdala appears for the first time in Luke 8. Mary is identified along with a group of other women. All these women had been healed of sickness or freed from demons. However, what caused these women to stand out from other women in the gospels was that they supported Jesus and his disciples financially.

Though it was not unheard of for women in the first century to give financial support to a rabbi, it would have been extremely rare. Very few women had financial resources of their own. Most women could not own property, nor could they have careers. Financially, the average woman utterly depended upon her husband or other male relative.

Of the three women named in Luke 8:1-3, Mary of Magdala, Joanna, and Susanna, only Joanna is mentioned to have a husband. We do not know if Mary or Susanna had a spouse. In this case, the absence of mention makes for a strong case that neither were married.

Because women could not own land or hold jobs in first-century Palestine, the absence of a husband for these two women made them a rarity in their world. It appears that they had secured financial security for themselves. Single, financially secure women in first-century Palestine were as ordinary as a snowstorm in May.

The Role of Women in First-Century Palestine

Jewish women in the first century were considered little more than property of the men in their lives. This doesn't mean girls were not loved by their parents or that wives weren't loved by their husbands. It was simply the social status of women at the time.

The station of women was more than just oppressive from a financial standpoint. A woman's word carried no weight in legal matters and could not give testimony. Women were not allowed to enter the Temple proper but were restricted to the Court of Women just outside the Temple. At mealtimes, women would first serve the men and only eat once they had completed their meals. In the first century, Palestine was very much a patriarchal society.

The role of women in ancient Palestine makes Mary of Magdala's role in the gospels even more impactful. It also makes her portrayal outside of the New Testament since Pope Gregory even more ironic.

Mary's role in the gospels appears to be one of liberation. Mary and the women accompanying her at the crucifixion and resurrection are put on equal footing, if not more significant, than the apostles. Mary and her companions become the first witnesses to the resurrection and the apostles to the apostles.

Mary symbolizes liberation for Christian women everywhere, as an apostle to the apostle. That makes Mary of Magdala the very first Christian preacher, a role out of reach for many women even today. Mary stands as an example of what Christ desires as the role of women in the church and the world.

Mary of Magdala's Role in the Crucifixion and Resurrection

Each of the gospels tells a slightly different version of the crucifixion story. These differences are NOT due to the writers remembering the events differently but to offer different theological perspectives on Jesus' death. Matthew and Mark agree that upon Jesus' arrest, all the disciples ran away. Luke and John leave out this detail and focus on Peter's denial of Jesus in the courtyard of Caiaphas, the high priest's home.

Despite the differences in the gospel accounts of the crucifixion, there is a consistent detail throughout all of them. The women who followed Jesus were present at the execution of Christ. Of the four gospels, only Luke fails to name Mary of Magdala as a witness, instead using the vague "But all his acquaintances, including the women who had followed him from Galilee, stood at a distance, watching these things." Luke 23:49 (NRSV) to identify the witnesses.

The importance of the women being witnesses to the crucifixion cannot be overstated. Jesus' disciples fled, and Simon Peter denied even knowing Jesus, leaving Jesus abandoned. Not entirely; the women had remained faithful where the male disciples had stumbled.

The gospel writers were very sophisticated; details were not added without purpose. Every detail mattered to the story these writers were working to tell. Mary Magdalene being named as a witness to the crucifixion serves a purpose to the message of these gospels. That message, in part, is that women are essential contributors to the Kingdom of God. This type of faithfulness is what the church will be built upon.

Mary's presence at the crucifixion demonstrated her unshakable devotion to following Jesus. When the disciples fled after Jesus' arrest, they testified to just how dangerous it was to be a follower of Jesus at the time. Each of Jesus' followers risked arrest, imprisonment, torture, and even death. Mary and her fellow women's devotion in the face of danger was an example for persecuted Christians in the decades and centuries to follow.

The gospel writers make their most powerful statement on the role of women in God's kingdom and the church by naming Mary of Magdala as a witness to the resurrection. The resurrection is the defining moment in Christianity. The church does not exist without resurrection, and salvation is not assured. All four gospel writers list Mary of Magdala as one of the first witnesses to the most critical event in history.

In Mary's world, women could not testify in court. Given the choice, it would have made more sense for the gospel writers to list one or more male disciples as the witnesses to Jesus' resurrection. Yet, all four gospel writers name women.

Naming women as witnesses to this crucial event rejects society's accepted social structure. The gospel writers make it clear that this new religion would bring with it a counterculture where gender was no longer an obstacle to equality. This statement is just as controversial today as 2,000 years ago.

Mary Gets Her Voice

We now come to John 20:11-18, Mary's encounter with Jesus after the resurrection. Shockingly, in these eight verses, the only recorded words Mary of Magdala in any of the gospels are spoken. It seems strange that a woman who has been the subject of so much speculation and had so much influence for two millennia only speaks four sentences in all of the gospels.

In these four sentences, John puts an exclamation point on the power of the resurrection. John achieves this masterfully, using the setting of the encounter to his full advantage. Everything about this encounter speaks to the new world that Jesus' resurrection sets into motion.

The scene begins with Mary weeping at the empty tomb. Two angels ask her why she is weeping. Mary replies, "They have taken away my Lord, and I do not know where they have laid him."

Mary's response is one of a person still living in a pre-resurrection world. For Mary, the world was still one under the power of sin and death. Death was the natural and expected conclusion to a person's life.

Mary then turned and saw Jesus standing there. Yet she does not recognize him. Theologians have speculated that something different about Jesus' resurrected body prevented him from being recognized immediately. This phenomenon also occurs in Luke 24 as

Jesus travels with two followers on the road to Emmaus.

John then tells us that Mary had mistaken Jesus for the gardener. John wants us to begin thinking of the creation story in Genesis. By connecting the resurrection to the Garden of Eden, we learn that the resurrection is a new beginning. Not just a new beginning, but a restoration.

Jesus speaks Mary's name, and instantly, she recognizes him. This can be seen as a parallel to God speaking the world into existence. Genesis has two different creation stories. The first is in Genesis 1:1-2:4. The second creation story takes place in Genesis 2:5-3:24. In the first creation story, God speaks humanity into existence, both male and female.

When Jesus speaks Mary's name at the resurrection, she is recreated. The world is put back right. Women are no longer subservient to men but, once again, a partner. This is how God intended the world to be, as illustrated in Genesis:

> *Then the Lord God said, "It is not good that the man should be alone; I will make him a helper as his partner."*
>
> **Genesis 2:18 (NRSV)**

For far too long, women had been silenced. The resurrection of Jesus gave voice to the voiceless. In the 20th chapter of John, Jesus does not simply allow Mary to speak; he commands her to speak. Jesus calls Mary to bear witness to his resurrection.

The word "apostle" comes from the Greek "Apostolos," which means one sent on a mission. Mary was sent on a mission. She was to carry the news of Jesus' resurrection to the eleven remaining disciples. Mary was the apostle to the apostles. Without Mary, the disciples would have remained in hiding and may never have found the courage to preach the Good News. Peter may have been the rock on which Christ built his church, but Mary was the lever Jesus used to move that rock into place.

Conclusion

The gospel writers worked very hard to show Mary of Magdala as an example of women's role in the new creation. The portrayal of Mary as a prostitute over the centuries and the misreading of passages from the Apostle Paul, such as 1 Corinthians 14:34 and 1 Timothy 2:12, have hindered Mary's impact.

Today, too many women are denied the opportunity to preach. Women in the United States still make $ 0.70 on the dollar of what men make in the same position. The role and status of women in many third-world countries remain a human rights violation. The world and the church have a long way to go to live into Christ's new creation.

The church needs to reignite the message in the Mary of Magdala's story. Her story should inspire the church to speak out for women's rights everywhere. Churches that are hesitant or outright resistant to accepting a female pastor would do well to remember who the preacher of the Good News was. If Christ can send a woman to spread the word, we should at least be able to accept hearing the word from a woman.

Jesus gave voice to Mary of Magdala so that every voiceless person might be heard. As a man and a person to whom society has given a voice, it is my call as a follower of Christ to listen to those with no voice. What role will you play to ensure that Mary and every other voiceless person is heard?

Reflection Questions

Outside of the Bible, where have you seen Mary Magdalene mentioned?

How has Mary been presented in secular sources?

What does Mary's inclusion in ancient gnostic gospels tell us about her place in the early church?

What are some of the similarities between the story of the sinful woman in Luke 7, and Mary of Bethany in John 12? How are they different?

How has the role of women in society and the church changed in the last 2,000 years? How has it remained relatively unchanged?

What does Mary's role as an apostle to the apostles mean to you?

What was the difference between the disciples' response to Jesus' arrest and the women's response?

Why do you think John chose to connect Mary's encounter with the risen Jesus with the creation stories found in Genesis?

How does Mary of Magdala inspire you?

From the book, *Ten Adult Sunday School Lessons by Clergy of the Holston Conference*, 2024.

BONUS LESSON

There is Yet Hope
Lesson by Walter Cross

About the lesson writer:

Walter Cross answered the call to preach in 1992. He attended Emory University, Candler School of Theology in Atlanta, Georgia, completing Pastoral Course of Study. He serves as a mentor for candidates pursuing ministry in the United Methodist Church. Pastor Cross lives in Knoxville, Tennessee, and is the husband of The Reverend Dr. Angela Hardy Cross.

Scripture Lesson:
Romans 4:18-25

> *Against all hope, Abraham in hope believed and so became the father of many nations, just as it had been said to him, "So shall your offspring be." Without weakening in his faith, he faced the fact that his body was as good as dead—since he was about a hundred years old—and that Sarah's womb was also dead. Yet he did not waver through unbelief regarding the promise of God, but was strengthened in his faith and gave glory to God, being fully persuaded that God had power to do what he had promised. This is why "it was credited to him as righteousness." The words "it was credited to him" were written not for him alone, but also for us, to whom God will credit righteousness—for us who believe in him who raised Jesus our Lord from the dead. He was delivered over to death for our sins and was raised to life for our justification.*
>
> **Romans 4:18-25 (NIV)**

A Lesson About Hope from My Mother

It was a pleasant Saturday in autumn in the middle of the 1950s, and I was just a wee little tike. My assignment in that early morning was to assist my mother in preparing food for the church's annual homecoming meal.

My father had recently deposited a ten-pound bag of sweet potatoes in the kitchen, along with a bushel of green beans. I was assigned to help my mother with the prep work, so I scraped the sweet potatoes, which she later cut up and put in a big pot of water to boil. I really wasn't that much help. My mother could have done the job all by herself, but she was helping to entertain me on a Saturday. She knew how to take a green bean, snap it, and pull that long string off it. I could snap a green bean, but my string would always tear off.

The end result of the basket that went to the church the next day was a layer of aluminum foil on the bottom, covered by a clean kitchen towel. My mother transformed those ten pounds of potatoes into four delicious sweet potato pies. I saw every one of them when they went in the oven and when they came out. She used real butter—not margarine like we usually got. They smelled like vanilla, nutmeg, ginger, and all the delicious ingredients.

Next to the pies were two chickens. Two fryers cut up, plus six extra wings. My mother would fry the chicken to perfection in an old black skillet till those caramelized brown pieces would form on the bottom. She would flip the chicken over so easily, with no flash, no pop. That was layer one: the warm layer.

Next, there was a cool layer. On Sunday morning, she put a layer of ice, then twenty-four deviled eggs. Of course, we couldn't take deviled eggs to church, so we called them angel eggs. On top of the angel eggs was a tray of carrots, sweet pickles, and a relish tray. The relish tray had celery, creamed cheese, and little bitty olives.

Next to that tray was a group of toothpicks with Vienna sausages, stuffed olives, and a cube of cheese. They were all lined up like little soldiers. That was the cool layer. She covered that with aluminum foil and another insulating towel.

I got to look at all that food, and then it all went to the preacher's table right after church that Sunday afternoon. I didn't get to eat with the group at the church. Instead, I sat with the organist in the sanctuary while he practiced. I was only five years old, and I would eat my meals at home.

My hope was—yes, there was hope—that there would be something left over from all that chicken and all those pies and all those green beans, that there would be something left for me. I lived in hope. But as the time passed that Sunday, hope began to wane. The preachers were hungry. They asked for seconds. They asked for thirds. Then, they asked for some to take home.

When I went to take the baskets to the car, there was nothing left in the baskets but those towels and some crumpled aluminum foil. I was sad.

I sat in the back seat of the car, thinking, "I'm going to dine on bologna crackers tonight," which would have been okay if I hadn't seen all the fixings my mother had prepared for the meal. But I had seen all of that food.

- I saw all that chicken.
- I saw all those sweet potato pies.
- I saw the green beans.
- I saw all the fixings my mother had made and those homemade brown-and-serve rolls.

And there I sat with an empty basket. My hope was crushed. I sat silently as we went home.

Mother: Walter, Junior. Are you alright?

Me: Yes, ma'am.

Father: Boy, what's wrong with you?

Me: I'm okay, Dad.

I went into the house and sat at the table, anticipating my bologna crackers. My mother looked at me. She almost smiled, but she kept a stern look. She opened the oven. In the back of the oven was pie number five, three chicken wings, and a corner piece of cornbread. Oh, I was so happy.

She looked at me again and said, You thought you got

left out. Always remember, there is something for you at home. There is always something for you at home. Patience helps develop hope.

The Hopeless Situation of the Romans

When I turn in my Bible to Romans, the writer is dealing with a situation plaguing the Christians. There's an influx of culture there. The Greek culture and the Roman culture. There's this new movement called "The Way" and a myriad of doctrines, and sometimes it left the new Christians confused. The Old Testament scholars wanted them to adhere strictly to the law. It turns out that the law was neither a friend to them nor a friend to us.

So, Paul steps in and says, "I need to explain something to you all. You all are in a hopeless situation because you've found out you can't keep the law. You're being terrorized by individuals in the religious community who are forcing the law upon you, and they know that you can't keep it because they can't keep it. Your situation appears to be hopeless."

Paul comes to the rescue in Romans, Chapter 8, the rescue chapter for hopeless Christians. Paul gives a list of items that are difficult to deal with:

> *I consider that our present sufferings are not worth comparing with the glory that will be revealed in us. For the creation waits in eager expectation for the children of God to be revealed. For the creation was subjected to*

frustration, not by its own choice, but by the will of the one who subjected it, in hope that the creation itself will be liberated from its bondage to decay and brought into the freedom and glory of the children of God.

We know that the whole creation has been groaning as in the pains of childbirth right up to the present time. Not only so, but we ourselves, who have the first fruits of the Spirit, groan inwardly as we wait eagerly for our adoption to sonship, the redemption of our bodies.

Romans 8:18-23 (NIV)

There is yet hope

Then, in verse 24, Paul says, "There is yet hope. Hope is not something that you can see."

There are two types of hope in the Bible and two types of hope in our lives today. I may hope to win the lottery one day—I don't know how because I don't play the lottery. Winning the lottery is a hope that is defined by chance.

I hope I get a good grade. I hope *Publishers Clearing House* stops by my home and knocks on the door. I hope I get that new car.

That's not what Paul is talking about.

In the New Testament, the word "hope" means *a certainty*. It means it is already done. It means God has handled the situation for us.

Hymn author Edward Mote said it well in 1834:

*My hope is built on nothing less
than Jesus' blood and righteousness;*

*I dare not trust the sweetest frame,
but wholly lean on Jesus' name.*[1]

My salvation is done by the finished work on Calvary. I don't hope to be saved. I am. I don't hope to go to Heaven. I'm on my way. Not because of my goodness. It's because—as Paul says—there is nothing remaining that can separate me from the love of God.

*On Christ, the solid Rock, I stand:
all other ground is sinking sand;
all other ground is sinking sand.*

Can anything ever separate us from Christ's love? Does it mean he no longer loves us if we have trouble or calamity, or are persecuted, or hungry, or destitute, or in danger, or threatened with death? (As the scriptures say, "For your sake we are killed every day; we are being slaughtered like sheep.") No, despite all these things, overwhelming victory is ours through Christ, who loved us.

> *And I am convinced that nothing can ever separate us from God's love. Neither death nor life, neither angels nor demons, neither our fears for today nor our worries about tomorrow—not even the powers of hell can separate us from God's love. No power in the sky above or in the earth below—indeed, nothing in all creation will ever be able to separate us from the love of God that is revealed in Christ Jesus our Lord.*
>
> **Romans 8:35-39 (NIV)**

Not peril, not destruction, not even the idea that we

---

1 Hymn: My Hope is Built, *United Methodist Hymnal* #368.

stand on this moment at the brink of World War III. That won't separate me. Not because of the scourge of this dreaded disease that has been sweeping our world for the last few years. Not the crisis in Israel and Gaza. Not the battle between Ukraine and Russia.

That's not going to separate me from the love of God.

- Racism is not going to separate me.
- Hateful speech is not going to separate me.
- Who's president is not going to separate me.
- Who's not the president is not going to separate me.
- What's happening in my family—what's happening in my heart—will not separate me from the Love of God.

It's a done deal.

Reflection Questions

What situations or events in our nation and world make you sometimes feel hopeless?

Are there times when you've felt separated from God? If so, what were some of the causes of those feelings?

How does it make you feel to hear Paul insist there is nothing that can separate you from the love of God?

More Studies From Market Square

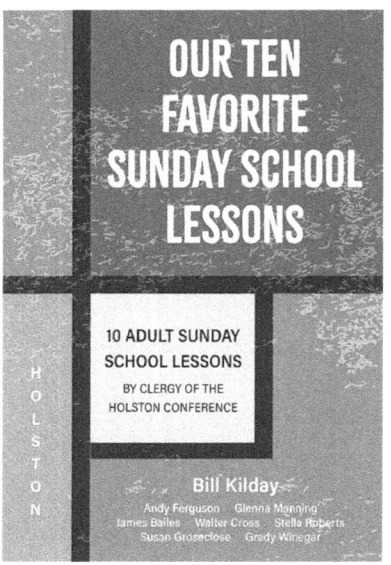
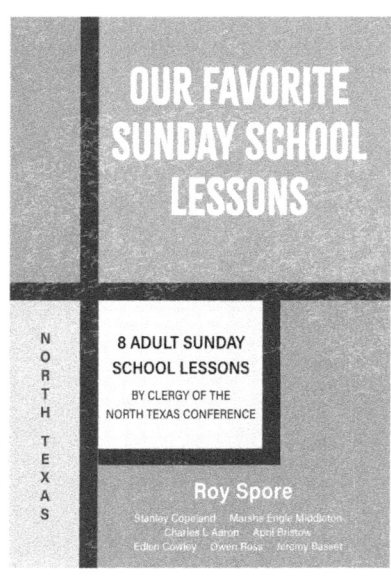
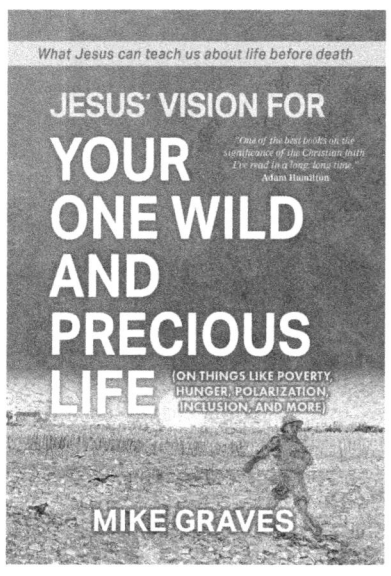
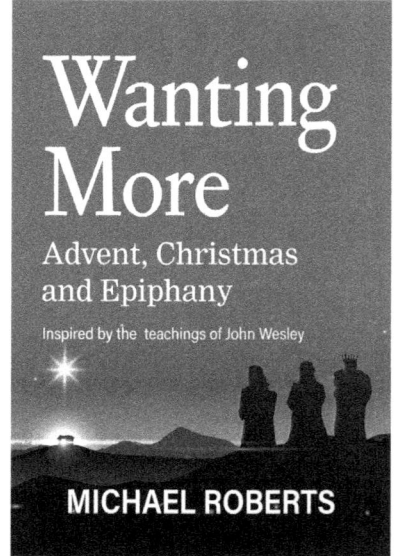

www.ingramcontent.com/pod-product-compliance
Lightning Source LLC
Chambersburg PA
CBHW061801070526
44586CB00023B/2662